WHO WAS JESUS?

WHO WAS JESUS?

by

COLIN CROSS

HODDER AND STOUGHTON

Printed in Great Britain for Hodder and Stoughton Limited, St. Paul's House, Warwick Lane, London, E.C.4, by Ebenezer Baylis and Son Limited, The Trinity Press, Worcester, and London

For

David Astor

Contents

Introduction

In approaching this difficult subject I have tried to use a spirit of detachment and journalistic inquiry. My aim has not been to set out any new theory of that remarkable figure, Jesus of Nazareth, but merely to try to establish an irreducible minimum of fact about him. Many, basing themselves upon religious faith, upon specialised scholarship, upon imaginative speculation or upon all three, would claim that a good deal more can be known about Jesus than I state. However, such people tend to disagree with each other, often very radically. I have no technical qualifications at all — I read neither Hebrew nor Greek — but I have attempted to use standard journalistic techniques in trying to trace what is common ground among most mainstream scholars. I have also tried to indicate one or two points of comparison between Jesus and other major religious figures.

My method, in the first place, is to avoid the use of the microscope. Viewed from a distance and considered as a whole, Jesus of Nazareth is a reasonably tangible historical figure. But too close an examination of any individual detail of him causes him to blur. One thinks of a coarse screen newspaper illustration which is made up of hundreds of tiny blobs of ink. The illustration as a whole is recognisable but a magnifying glass reduces it to meaningless blobs. The reason for uncertainty about Jesus is the simplest possible. It is just that there is no record at all, of any kind, about the greater part of his life. He wrote no book. Even what he looked like is unknown. There is not a word of independent proof that he ever

even existed. The records that do exist, the gospels, cover only
a fraction of Jesus's life and are written from a cultic and
ritualistic point of view and not as ordinary history. There are
the gravest inconsistencies in the gospel accounts and also
many blatant improbabilities.

Of course this serious shortage of information about Jesus
has in some sense actually added to his stature as a religious
personality. Many different people in many different cultures
have been able to make up their own idea of Jesus, with a minimum of obstruction from fact. The disparities are absurdly
wide, even in our own day. I know advocates of non-violence
who claim Jesus as their leading inspiration. Also I have
attended a religious service at which accredited clergy blessed
a Polaris weapons system in Jesus's name. Some people use
the name of Jesus to endorse the capitalist system. Others talk
about him as if he were some kind of early socialist. It is commonly reckoned, without a shred of proof, that he was a poor
man. There was even, for a time, a sort of Nazi Jesus. To many
today Jesus is an infinitely kind and loving friend. But at least
until very recently he was also presented as an appallingly
severe judge who inflicted infinitely cruel punishments. Such
attempts to 're-interpret Jesus to the needs of our own day'
are at best unhistorical and at worst sheer slop. Such other
comparable religious geniuses as the Buddha and Mahomet
are capable of being treated as real historical personalities.
There seems to be no reason to suppose that the great Jesus
deserves less.

Having decided that the only way to get at the historical
Jesus is to look at him as a whole and against the broadest
possible background, one finds oneself covering a thousand
years of history. The natural starting point is the prophet
Deutero-Isaiah who in about 550 B.C. defined and proclaimed
a vivid idea of God which, at least until very recently, was
the cornerstone alike of the Jewish, Christian and Islamic
faiths. Recent thought about the nature of this God has
tended somewhat to depersonalise him and this is the greatest

revolution in theology since Deutero-Isaiah. However, the
God of Jesus was the God of Deutero-Isaiah. The preachings,
speculations and inspirations of Deutero-Isaiah and his successors produced a thriving Jewish theological system which
formed the entire background to Jesus's life and thought.

It is crucial to get over the point that the Judaism which
produced Jesus was not the same as Judaism of the Old
Testament. Nor was it the same as the Judaism of today.
Progressive, sectarian Jews, of whom Jesus was one, had their
own oral traditions covering such central matters as the
resurrection of the dead, angels and demons, ritual meals,
baptism and the nature of the special leader, the Christ, to be
sent by God. For their own reasons, later Jewish and Christian leaders tended to cover up, censor or even falsify some of
the elements of the sectarian Judaism of the first century B.C.
and this process, as one of its side-effects, obliterated much of
the historical character of Jesus. In the last twenty years,
however, with the discovery of the Dead Sea scrolls—that is
documents written by a Jewish sect in the first century A.D.—
the period has begun seriously to be looked at for the first
time. Scholarship is advancing so rapidly that detailed books
on the subject become out of date nearly as rapidly as text-
books on advanced physics. However the outline seems to be
reasonably clear and it is certainly absolutely essential for
even beginning to understand Jesus. The major point is that
Jesus and the early Christians were much more purely Jewish
than had previously been supposed. To take angels, for
example, they were not a doctrine made up by Jesus. They
existed in sectarian Judaism and were swallowed whole, and
without effort, by the Christian sect.

The two outstanding doctrines were those of the resurrection of the dead and of the coming of the Christ.

There are only the slightest scraps of support in the Old
Testament for the doctrine of the resurrection of the dead and
many Jews in Jesus's time did not believe in it. However the
'progressives', Jesus among them, thoroughly accepted it.

They really thought dead people were going to climb out of their graves. No idea could be more exciting. It is against this background, I suggest, that the claim that Jesus came back from the dead should be examined. Little profit is to be derived from detailed examination of the inconsistent New Testament accounts of the subject or from speculating on the improbability that Jesus managed to survive crucifixion without dying. What matters is that people were continually or frequently thinking about dead men coming back to life and that when miracles are expected to happen they frequently do appear to happen. The idea of Jesus being resurrected was more credible to Jewish sectarians than it is to a twentieth century agnostic. Indeed, by the Matthew account, not only Jesus was resurrected but also many other 'holy men'.[1] To understand Jesus it is necessary to understand that he believed in the resurrection of the dead in the most literal way. It was not an idea he made up himself but one which he absorbed in his studies of Judaism.

The idea of the Christ was more definitely foreshadowed in the Old Testament but Jewish sects had their own various and elaborate oral and written traditions on the subject. The Essenes, for example, believed that there would be two Christs. The common ground was that the Christ (or Messiah) was to be a miraculous leader sent by God. In my view the original Christians were a sect of Jews who had their own special ideas about the Christ. This sect (like others) believed that it was acting under the direct inspiration of God. Ultimately, unlike some others, it felt inspired to preach its doctrines outside the Jewish community and so, ultimately, became a separate religion. In the beginning it was an essentially forward-looking group, expecting the coming of the Christ and the cosmic revolution in the near future. The exact relationship of the historical Jesus of Nazareth to this group is far from clear. Obviously in his own day Jesus did not make much public impact and the major growth of the group came only after his death. However, as time passed

the group continued to look back upon him as its founder
and to believe that it had mystical communication with him.
A modern secular parallel might be that of Karl Marx. In
his own lifetime, Marx was not an outstandingly important
figure; his death passed with little comment and only about
six people attended his funeral. However the movements of
which he was a member expanded after his death on a
gigantic scale and more and more he came to be looked back
to as the father figure and, almost, as a god. He was moved
out of his original grave into a more prominent one, with a
big image of him on it; pictures, statues and busts of him
proliferate across the world. One is tempted to press the
analogy further and claim that Lenin was to Marx as Paul
of Tarsus was to Jesus; however the analogy is admittedly
fragile and not too much weight should be placed upon it.
In the case of Jesus and the Christians, the original claim
seems to have been that in Jesus the Christ had made a preliminary appearance on earth already and was at any
moment going to return properly with full power. Later,
when this had failed to happen, the mystical Jesus in heaven
was given increasing status and ultimately defined as God.
Also Jesus's career on earth, which in the first days had not
seemed particularly important compared with his imminent
return, attracted more and more interest. Paul of Tarsus,
who seems to have been the great pioneer in taking the Christ
doctrine to non-Jews, did not, according to his letters, preach
about the earthly Jesus at all. However it was not too long
before accounts of the life and teachings of Jesus were being
read out at Christian services.

On the whole I think it reasonable to suppose that the
reports of words spoken by Jesus, although written long after
his death, contain a substantial degree of accuracy. They
have been subjected to editing and to interpolation but, taken
as a whole, they do in at least a rough and ready way give
some indication of the kind of person Jesus was and how he
thought. My own, subjective induction is that he was a

vehement man with some sense of humour. He knew a lot of theology and, in terms of the Judaism of his time, was well educated. On both doctrine and morals he said very little that was new. His enormous skill was as a propagandist. He may well have possessed apparent psychic powers and skills in healing—such things were not uncommon in sectarian Judaism. Certainly any attempt to strip Jesus of his miraculous element so as to make him more palatable to modern Christians is to distort history. If Jesus of Nazareth believed in anything at all, he believed in miracles.

Having started the book with Deutero-Isaiah and taken it into Jesus's own milieu of sectarian Judaism it was necessary to find a logical conclusion. I have a prejudice against accounts of great men which stress merely their intellectual and other defects without also explaining the special skills and talents which enabled them to make their mark. In the case of Jesus, his real mark on history came after his death. A very energetic and charismatic group, containing many remarkable personalities, spread faith in him throughout the Roman Empire. It would seem to be impossible to make sense of Jesus without taking this group fully into account. Apart from anything else, it is not possible to read the gospels sensibly without knowing a little about the people who wrote and propagated them. The natural end of the book, therefore, seemed to be the Council of Nicea in A.D. 325 which formally defined the divinity of Jesus and, also, marked Christianity's emergence as a major world religion.

This book is journalistic not only in its method but also in its origin. It grew originally out of assignments for the Hon. David Astor, Editor of *The Observer*, and Mr. John Thompson, Editor of *The Observer Magazine*; I would like to thank them deeply both for pushing me into a field I would not otherwise have entered and for their continual encouragement and stimulation. I am grateful to *The Observer*, Ltd., for permission to reproduce certain passages which are their copyright.

The English of my scriptural quotations, except where otherwise stated, is that of the Jerusalem Bible.

I have added a short bibliography, made up rather subjectively of books that I have found particularly interesting or valuable.

Colin Cross

[1] Mt 27: 52

I

The Empty Room

JESUS of Nazareth was a Galilean Jew of the first century A.D.
He was a religious visionary and, for a short time, a preacher.
Upon the tradition of his personality was founded Christianity which, in terms of numbers of adherents, is the biggest
religion in the history of the world: today some 950 million
people live in countries belonging to the Christian tradition.
Yet most of the elementary biographical facts about Jesus are
either unknown or a subject for scholarly controversy. Even
what he looked like is unknown. He is thus an infinitely more
mysterious figure than such other founders of world religions
as the Buddha or Mahomet, both of whose biographies are
known to a fair degree of certainty. The obscurity of Jesus's
personality and life have, it seems, actually encouraged his
cult; people of many different cultures and civilisations have
put into Jesus what they wanted to believe about him, with
little obstruction from facts. The religious instinct is a part of
human nature and one which Jesus has fitted very well.

Yet although there have been an almost infinite number of
different kinds of Jesus preached to the public (over 60,000
books are said to have been written about him in the last
century alone), there does somewhere seem to be a real man
behind them all. A secular parallel, perhaps, is the playwright
William Shakespeare, biographical information about whom
is so sparse that it has been seriously questioned whether he
existed as a writer at all. However, the 'works of Shakespeare'
exist, whoever wrote them, and in the same way the parables
and preachings of Jesus exist whatever their precise origin.

Moreover it is possible to get a reasonable understanding of Shakespeare's life by studying the English theatre of the sixteenth century and the kind of people who were successful in it. Similarly, the starting point for the study of Jesus must be an examination of the context in which he lived and won supporters.

That he was a Jew of the first century meant that he belonged to a tumultuous, fruitful community which was at the most exciting moment in its history. First century Judaism, with its sects arguing furiously with each other, was probably the most potent religious movement that has ever existed. It was the common ancestor of three world religions — Christianity, Islam and modern Judaism.

The Jews were partly a nation and partly a religious faith; if they are dated from Moses, they are by far the oldest world religion. Exact figures about their strength are impossible to establish but there were probably about four million of them in the time of Jesus and they formed possibly seven per cent of the population of the Roman Empire, which was then the political master of the Mediterranean world. About half the total lived in the territories of Judaea and Galilee in what can conveniently be described as Palestine, although that term was not yet in use: their religious capital which contained their Temple was Jerusalem in Judaea. The remainder were scattered widely across the Roman Empire and beyond. They were a prominent community, well organised and attractive to converts. They were a recognised factor in the world. So far as analogies with the twentieth century are possible, they can be compared to the Roman Catholics in today's United States or Great Britain. That is they were a strong minority, with international connections, their own inner life and their own rules of conduct which did not always correspond with those of society at large. The Roman Empire, itself a highly religious organisation, classified Jews as 'atheists' because they repudiated the imperial gods and allowed them exemptions from public duties which involved contact with the worship of the gods. They could appear stiff and sticky and some non-members disliked them; but they attracted much interest and were winning many new members. Judaism was a proselytising religion. Apart from Palestine, the main centre was Alexandria, Egypt, where about a quarter of the population was Jewish. Another important centre was the city of Babylon which stood between the rivers Tigris and Euphrates outside the Roman Empire to the east.

In Jesus's time the Jewish religion was in a revolutionary phase and it was divided into many sects and schools of thought. Scholars argued with each other about the interpretation of the scriptures handed down from the past and about oral tradition. Some teachers claimed direct divine inspiration to override the interpretations of the scholars. It was a bubbling hot-pot of conflict and argument, spiced with stories of wonders and miracles, and everything seemed urgent and crucial because of the widely held belief among them that a miraculous personality, the Messiah, was about to appear and end the existing world order. Christianity itself started as a Jewish Messianic sect. The unifying link between the various Jewish sects was a belief in an all-powerful invisible God, Yahweh,* who had made the world and took an active interest in what its inhabitants were up to. Yahweh had given the Jews a special revelation of himself and a law by which they were to live.

Within this framework of belief in Yahweh there was room for the widest diversity and it would be false to suppose that the Judaism of Jesus's time was a settled, organic system like normative modern Judaism. Nothing is more misleading than the label applied by nineteenth century critics which described it as *Das Spätjudentum*—late Judaism. By any reasonable reckoning of chronology, there was nothing at all 'late' about it. Jewish teachers were contending with each other on the most fundamental questions. It was not even agreed

---

* The word 'Yahweh' up to the nineteenth century was normally expressed in English as 'Jehovah'.

whether individual human beings could survive death. It was another four centuries before editors in Babylon set out the Talmud, the collection of teachings at the basis of modern, normative Judaism, in its final form. To call the Judaism of the first century 'late Judaism' is like describing the Socialism of Karl Marx's day as 'late Socialism'. The Jewish tumult was so vigorous that it was almost certain to produce great results of some kind and, in fact, it produced the three world religions of modern Judaism, Christianity and Islam, each claiming to be the legitimate heir.

Worship of Yahweh as a potential world religion originated in the imperial city of Babylon in the sixth century B.C. This was a fruitful period of religious development in several parts of the world and, indeed, it can be reckoned that all the major world religions except Hinduism started almost simultaneously at this moment: it saw Prince Gautama, the Buddha (c. 566–486 B.C.) preaching in India, Confucius (551–479 B.C.) preaching in China, and Zoroaster (c. 598– 540 B.C.) founding the Parsees in Persia and putting out ideas which were to influence many other groups. The Greek philosophers Socrates and Plato lived about a century later. Unlike its fellows in other parts of the world, Judaism had no single founder but there is one personality who especially stands out, the author of the last twenty-six chapters of the Book of Isaiah. His name is lost and he is usually referred to as Deutero-Isaiah (second Isaiah). He was a Babylonian Jew flourishing in about 550 B.C. and he together, possibly, with followers who wrote the final chapters of the book, must be counted among the most influential men of all time. His eloquence flashes across the centuries with the germinative idea of Yahweh, the all-powerful God.

'. . . All the nations are as nothing in his presence, for him they count as nothingness and emptiness. To whom could you liken God? What image could you contrive of him? . . . He lives above the circle of the earth, its inhabitants look like grasshoppers. He has stretched out the heavens like a cloth, spread them like a tent for men to live in . . . Yahweh is an everlasting God, he created the boundaries of the earth. . .'[1]

This supreme force, according to Deutero-Isaiah, was interested in human welfare and could provide comfort.

'. . . Here is the Lord Yahweh coming with power . . . He is like a shepherd feeding his flock, gathering lambs in his arms, holding them against his breast and leading to their rest the mother ewes . . . Young men may grow tired and weary, youths may stumble, but those who hope in Yahweh will renew their strength, they put out wings like eagles. They run and do not weary, walk and never tire . . .'[2]

Then Yahweh, too, was the God for the whole world and would punish people who did not accept him.

'. . . Am I not Yahweh? There is no other God besides me, a God of integrity and a saviour. Turn to me and be saved, all the ends of the earth, for I am God unrivalled. By my own self I swear it; what comes from my mouth is truth, a word irrevocable: before me every knee shall bend, by me every tongue shall swear, saying "From Yahweh alone comes victory and strength" . . . All mankind will come to bow down in my presence, says Yahweh. And on their way out they will see the corpses of men who have rebelled against me. Their worm will not die nor their fire go out; they will be loathsome to all mankind.'[3]

Jesus of Nazareth must have been thoroughly acquainted with this book. Indeed as a boy he may well have learned the whole of it by heart. The God preached by Jesus was the God of Deutero-Isaiah. The personality of Yahweh, as developed in Babylon, was to form the basis of the religions of the west and it was quite distinct and different from the ideas that simultaneously were arising in the east. The Buddha had no God in his system; he taught that what mattered was to live in harmony with impersonal cosmic forces. Confucius saw the highest ideal in the sane, decent administration of a political community, producing the 'superior man' marked by humanity, wisdom and courage. Of course both the Buddha and Confucius, and for that matter Deutero-Isaiah and the Greek philosophers, were acting against a strong popular prejudice in favour of a multitude of deities and mysterious powers; to go with an intellectual demand for what can be termed the higher forms of religion, there was a popular demand for idols. The Jewish genius, typified by Deutero-Isaiah, was to channel the hunger for deities into the adoration of the single, all-powerful Yahweh, who was a warm, personal being with a definite programme for the world and who could be influenced by prayer, sacrifice and virtuous behaviour. It was possible to hope to persuade Yahweh to do things and, even, to argue with him. As the 39th Psalm, addressed to Yahweh, puts it: 'Look, you have given me an inch or two of life, my life span is nothing to you; each man that stands on earth is only a puff of wind, every man that walks, only a shadow, and the wealth he amasses is only a puff of wind—he does not know who will take it next. So tell me, Lord, what can I expect? My hope is in you . . . Lay your scourge aside, I am worn out with the blows you deal me . . .'[4] As the future was to show, such a conception of a personal God harmonised with many human instincts: it was a powerful idea which was profoundly to influence the western world and still in the twentieth century is the subject of much thought. It was, however, an idea that needed vigorously to be preached; the Yahweh-type deity cannot be regarded as a norm of human belief—most people in most places at most times have not accepted it.

Who were these people in Babylon in the sixth century B.C. who propounded Yahweh as the universal deity?

They can, for convenience, be termed Jews, although, strictly, that word was not yet in use. For centuries they had run their own kingdoms in Palestine. They looked back in their traditions to a patriarch called Abraham (c. 1800 B.C.), to a leader called Moses (c. 1250 B.C.) who had led them out of captivity in Egypt, to a king called David (c. 1000 B.C.), who had established their community on a firm basis and to another king, Solomon (*c.* 950 B.C.) who had built the first temple to Yahweh in Jerusalem. In conflict with the Babylonians under King Nebuchadnezzar, who reigned 604–562 B.C., they had been conquered and in successive deportations the leading members of the community had been exiled to Babylon, about 600 miles from their homeland. Such deportations were Nebuchadnezzar's normal means of consolidating a conquest.

Up to this point the invisible Yahweh had been only a tribal god, that is he was supposed to fight for the tribe against the gods of other tribes, and, moreover, the Jews had been far from strictly monotheistic. As the prophet Jeremiah had put it immediately before the defeat '... You have as many gods as you have towns, Judah, as many incense altars for Baal as Jerusalem has streets.'[5] The crucial development in Babylon was that in the face of utter disaster the leading exiles did not blame Yahweh or lose faith in him. The disaster was a punishment from Yahweh for their sins. If they ascertained and obeyed the will of Yahweh they would be restored to their homeland for Yahweh was powerful enough to do anything he wanted.

Thus it was in Babylon that the Jews set about editing and consolidating their tribal history and traditions, covering a time-span as long as that between the reigns of King Alfred the Great and Queen Elizabeth II. The resulting documents form the greater part of the Old Testament, which is a combination of history, theology and poetry, much of it reaching the highest literary and moral levels. Undoubtedly there is a good deal of real history in the Old Testament and many of the episodes are consistent with modern archaeological research, although, unfortunately, there is no independent confirmation of Moses and the escape from Egypt. The Babylonian exiles made such a valuable and influential compilation in the Old Testament that it is a temptation to quote from it here at great length but, perhaps, the 15th Psalm can suffice as expressing as well as anything else the power of the

Jewish tradition at its most sober. It is short enough to be
given in full:

> 'Yahweh, who has the right to enter your tent,
> or to live on your holy mountain?
> The man whose way of life is blameless,
> who always does what is right,
> who speaks the truth from his heart,
> whose tongue is not used for slander,
> who does no wrong to his fellow,
> casts no discredit on his neighbour,
> looks with contempt on the reprobate,
> but honours those who fear Yahweh;
> who stands by his pledge at any cost,
> does not ask interest on loans,
> and cannot be bribed to victimise the innocent.
> —If a man does all this, nothing can ever shake him.'

Babylon under Nebuchadnezzar was a great metropolitan
centre and materially the Jews flourished there. They were
allowed lands to cultivate and some of them rose to high
positions at court. They were in contact with a wide variety
of peoples, some, like themselves, compulsorily exiled. They
were at a cultural and economic crossroads. This, presumably,
had the effect of stimulating their thinking about Yahweh;
if he was to stand up against other people's deities he had to
be thought of in more cosmic terms than had been sufficient
in the rural backwater of Jerusalem. Also, in compiling some
of the Old Testament they drew upon the common stock of
Middle Eastern legends, especially those relating to the
earliest history of the human race. The creation and flood
stories in Genesis have their counterparts in non-Jewish
sources and it seems that the Jewish editors took them wholesale into their tradition: in the case of the creation they took
two different, and inconsistent, legends and just set them
out side by side to form the first two chapters of Genesis. Even
the basic moral code, the Ten Commandments, closely

resembles Assyrian, Hittite and Mesopotamian codes, although in this case the cross-fertilisation probably had come earlier than the Babylonian period. Another kind of influence was contemporary non-Jewish religious teaching in which Zoroaster is a particularly interesting figure. Zoroaster taught a cosmic battle between darkness and light, human immortality, divine judgment and the existence of heaven and hell. Although such doctrines appear only in the most tenuous form in the canonical Jewish scriptures they certainly, from the time of the Babylonian exile onwards, were prominent in Jewish oral tradition and from that they became a part of Christianity. It has even been suggested that the later Jewish party of Pharisees, to whose basic tradition Jesus of Nazareth belonged, derived its name from Zoroaster's followers the Parsees.

The Babylonian Jews not only had doctrines but, also, they set up an organisation which was to be crucial for the future. The organisation was the synagogue, a group of believers meeting for prayer, instruction and communal administration. This, so far as can be ascertained, was new in Mediterranean religious organisation. Hitherto religion had revolved around certain sites regarded as sacred or certain statues or images, often with priests acting as mediators between the gods and man. In Jerusalem the Jews had had their own temple and hereditary priesthood. But in Babylon it was realised that Yahweh being invisible and universal could be worshipped anywhere and so the synagogue came into existence. The word 'synagogue' means, strictly, the group of worshippers and it is applied only informally to the building in which they meet; a synagogue can meet anywhere and presumably in the earliest period did so entirely in private houses. The hereditary priesthood was prominent in the early organisation of synagogues but was not essential to it; the qualification for teaching in the synagogue was knowledge of the scriptures or, occasionally, a claim to special inspiration from Yahweh. Eventually there came into existence definite orders of scribes and rabbis, who were skilled teachers not mystical priests, and they were eventually to take over the leadership of Judaism. The development of the synagogue in Babylon provided an essential pattern for the future. It gave a flexibility to Judaism and its associated religions which persists to this day—the church and the mosque are both, basically, synagogue-type institutions. Moreover the form of synagogue worship—prayer, reading and instruction—was also of value in the future: even so mystical a rite as the Catholic mass is largely synagogal in its procedure.

At about the same time as the synagogue was developing in Babylon, the Buddha in India was setting up a different kind of framework. The Buddha's way was to found the Sangha, the order of monks; during his forty-five years' ministry he gave much of his attention to planning it and it continues until this day as the backbone of Buddhist organisation. The Sangha consists of men who either permanently or temporarily renounce the ordinary pleasures of the world, including sex and private property, for the purpose of improving their enlightenment on eternal matters. From the beginning it was an essential part of their vocation for them to act as teachers and missionaries. 'In the spirit and in the letter, make ye known the perfect, utterly pure, righteous life,' the Buddha instructed them. (He also started an order for women.)

The two forms of organisation—the synagogal, with its stress on lay people meeting together, and the monastic, with its stress on the creation of an élite—are distinct from each other but not necessarily incompatible. The Jews, to some extent, and later the Christians, to a considerable extent, added monasticism to their system. The Buddhists, with monks acting as pastors and teachers in local temples, took in some synagogal elements. It would be interesting to know to what extent, if any, the Jewish and Buddhist pioneers knew of each other and imitated each other. Certainly in the twentieth century, the expansion of the Buddhist religion can in part be accounted for by its adoption of some of the methods of Christian missionaries. Whether there was contact 2,000 years ago is impossible to establish: all that can be stated is that communications between India and the Middle East certainly existed.

To the synagogue structure, the Jews in Babylon added other safeguards for their faith and individuality. They observed purely family festivals in the home, notably the Seder meal in the spring which was a commemoration of the escape from Egypt. With its ceremonial with glasses of wine and unleavened bread and the head of the family stating: 'He who is hungry, let him eat with us', it was to be the basis of much future religious ritual, but the idea of major religious rites being part of family life and taking place in the home was to remain distinctively Jewish and not to go into Christianity or Islam. Then there was the Torah, a detailed code of teaching by which the pious Jew was to sanctify every part of his life. The Torah included routine prohibitions against such things as stealing and cheating and a range of idiosyncratic teachings which marked out Jews as different from other men. These special practices covered diet, resting on the seventh day of the week, and prayer. The distinctive mark of the male Jew was that he had been circumcised; this had a mystical significance and some rabbis came to hold that the blood shed in the operation had a cleansing or redeeming effect. Running through the whole of the Torah was the notion of an individual relationship between Yahweh and each member of the faith; Yahweh was not just a communal god but a deity for the individual. The 139th Psalm expresses the belief in his omniscience:

'Yahweh, you examine me and know me,
you know if I am standing or sitting,
you read my thoughts from far away,
whether I walk or lie down, you are watching,
you know every detail of my conduct . . .'[6]

Of course it is impossible to be precise on the dates of the various customs. Many of them dated back to before the Babylonian exile and others were developed afterwards; up to and beyond the time of Jesus of Nazareth, Judaism was a fluid, evolving faith. The central fact, however, is that the exile was the great shock which might have destroyed Judaism but instead set its adherents about codifying and expanding their ideas. It produced the great prophet Deutero-Isaiah. The Jews strengthened their identity and separated their faith from any necessary connection with a particular political context. If they were influenced by non-Jewish factions around them, they, in turn, were at least as influential. With their doctrine of Yahweh, their scriptures and their synagogues they must have attracted interest and, probably, also converts.

The compulsory exile lasted for half a century, from 587 to 538 B.C., and during it the more religious of the Jews pined for their homeland. Indeed with the passage of time, homesickness became greater rather than less. Codified religious doctrines made it definite that Palestine was the land Yahweh had promised to the Jews and this stood at the centre of the faith, as in the 137th Psalm.

> 'Beside the streams of Babylon
> we sat and wept
> at the memory of Zion,
> leaving our harps
> hanging on the poplars there . . .
> . . . Jerusalem if I forget you,
> may my right hand wither!
> May I never speak again
> if I forget you!
> If I do not count Jerusalem
> The greatest of my joys! . . .'[7]

The aspiration was not just a pious hope but a practical proposition. The Jews put their faith in King Cyrus of Persia, who was rapidly extending his territories through military victories. Cyrus, they hoped, would conquer Babylon and liberate them. Deutero-Isaiah presented Cyrus as the actual instrument of Yahweh, as 'the anointed one'. In 539 B.C. Cyrus did indeed conquer Babylon and the following year he issued an edict allowing Jews, and other exiles, to return to their homelands. He appears to have held Yahweh in some respect and specifically sponsored the rebuilding of the Jewish Temple in Jerusalem. The Jews remained, of course, under Persian sovereignty and Cyrus appointed a commissioner, Sheshbazzar, to rule over them.

Probably it was only a minority of the most zealous Jews who took advantage of the new freedom and returned to Jerusalem. The majority continued to make their home in Babylon and to flourish there; the process can be compared with modern Zionism among British or American Jews; actual settlement in the Holy Land being attractive only to a minority. Those who did go back were as much missionaries as returning exiles. The population at large had to be evangelised with the new doctrines and practices and the new stiffness that had been developed in Babylon. Supported by Persian political authority, and under a succession of brilliant leaders, priests and prophets — Ezra, Nehemiah, Haggai and Zechariah — the amplified Jewish religion began to spread. At one point there was a compulsory mass divorce in which Jewish men were forced to get rid of non-Jewish wives. Some resisted, in particular the Samaritans who definitely repudiated what they regarded as Babylonian innovations and regarded only the Pentateuch, the first five books of the Old Testament, as binding. The Samaritans attacked Jerusalem, and relations between them and mainstream Jews became bitter and remained bitter for dozens of generations. Indeed it was not until the twentieth century that the Samaritan remnant and the Jews really formed an understanding. The enmities between the two communities were such that when Jesus of Nazareth preached a parable about 'The Good

Samaritan' it had something of the impact of a modern Jewish rabbi preaching about 'The Good Nazi'. The setting up of synagogues and the persuading of ordinary people to follow the practices of the Torah was a process that took centuries and, indeed, was never fully completed. Palestine was the country of the Jews but it has never been a 100 per cent Jewish country.

After two centuries, Persian dominance was defeated by the Greek Alexander the Great and the Jews became a part, but an independent part, of Hellenistic culture. Alexander actually visited Jerusalem and talked to the Jewish leaders. The contacts were, again, a two-way process with the two sides influencing each other and the most religious Jews, the Pharisees, defining the religion of Yahweh more closely to meet the challenge of Greek philosophy. One idea which was entirely Jewish but gradually spread was that of the Sabbath — the seventh day of the week on which no Jew would work. Jewish communities spread out into the cities of the Greek world, taking with them the idea of Yahweh, and Greek settlers founded cities in Palestine. The great meeting place was Alexandria, the Egyptian port named after Alexander the Great, and it was in Alexandria that the Jewish scriptures were translated into Greek, the Septuagint. The purpose of the translation was a missionary one, to make Jewish ideas known to the outside world. It was the Septuagint, rather than the Hebrew originals, which came to be used by most Christians: the point is of some importance because the Septuagint was less than completely accurate — a word in Isaiah which in Hebrew means 'young woman' was rendered in the Greek as 'virgin' and came to be used to support the doctrine of the virgin birth of Jesus of Nazareth.

The Jews were cherishing great hopes of their future as Yahweh's chosen people and believed that in some sense they would become masters of the world. Some Jews took this in the allegorical sense of Yahweh eventually converting all peoples but others were more directly political and thought of a Jewish master-race. Deutero-Isaiah had been definite on the point: 'Strangers will be there to feed your flocks, foreigners as your ploughmen and vinedressers; but you, you will be named "priests of Yahweh", they will call you "ministers of our God". You will feed on the wealth of nations and array yourselves in their magnificence.'[8] With such a splendid future before them, it was difficult to tolerate the subordinate position of their Holy Land which, although allowed a degree of autonomy, was under ultimately alien rule. Things became intolerable when the Hellenistic King of Syria, Antiochus Epiphanes (175–163 B.C.), actually began to persecute Judaism. He polluted the Jewish Temple with sacrifices of pigs' flesh and tried to force ordinary Jews to do the same. Some resisted and were executed—so far as is known, they were the first-ever Jewish martyrs, that is people who were willing to die for a religious principle. In an outburst of both religious and nationalistic feeling—the story sounds astonishingly modern—the Jews rose successfully in revolt and set up their own independent 'Commonwealth of Judaea' under a priestly family, the Hasmoneans. (The dynasty is also known as the Maccabees after a nickname, Maccabee, meaning 'Hammer', attached to the first of them.)

Independent Judaea lasted for about a century, until 63 B.C., and so was only as long before the time of Jesus of Nazareth as is the reign of Queen Victoria from today. Old men would have been living in Jesus's childhood who remembered Jewish independence. The state had periods of considerable success, widening its frontiers and bringing in new peoples and converting them to Judaism. At some time during it there lived a mysterious figure known as the 'Teacher of Righteousness' who set up a new Jewish sect, the Essenes, which repudiated the Jerusalem Temple. He was eventually murdered by a priest in Jerusalem and his life and doctrines bear some resemblance to those of Jesus of Nazareth; indeed it has been argued that Jesus was not a real person at all but an imaginary figure with biographical details based upon the

Teacher of Righteousness. The full importance of this sect was not appreciated until after its library of scrolls, preserved in caves by the Dead Sea, was discovered in 1948. The Teacher of Righteousness was part of a general religious ferment which, in the long run, contributed towards the downfall of the Hasmonean commonwealth. The progressive, innovating party, the Pharisees (from which the Teacher of Righteousness was presumably an offshoot) wanted to make the state completely theocratic and, when they failed, were willing to co-operate with foreign rulers to bring it down. The dynasty itself was split with family feuds and in 63 B.C. when it was in a state of civil war the new power of the Roman Empire took Judaea under its suzerainty.

The Roman commander Pompey was inquisitive about this profoundly religious people. His troops arrived at Jerusalem, which was still resisting, and Pompey found he could make progress with the siege by attacking on Saturdays, the Sabbath. Under the rules of the Torah, as they had been worked out by scribes and rabbis, the defenders were allowed to defend their own persons on the Sabbath but they were not allowed to defend the walls. Their last stand took place on the Temple Mount. Pompey's soldiers broke through the walls on the Sabbath and began to slaughter the occupants, including the priests on duty. It was noticed that when one priest was killed, another would step forward impassively to continue the rite as if this were ordinary routine. When the fighting was over, Pompey inspected the Temple and for a man of his Roman background it must have been a mysterious place. It was a centre for worship and sacrifice but contained no obvious god. It was bare of images or statues. He looked at the altar and at the Holy Place, which was ornamented with a seven-branched candlestick. Then he approached the curtain, ornamented probably with astrological symbols, which veiled off the inmost shrine, the Holy of Holies. This was where the Jewish God, Yahweh, dwelt, he had been told, and only the High Priest was allowed to enter. Pompey pulled aside the curtain and walked in. He found that it was just a small, windowless and empty room, probably rather dusty. For a moment he just stood there, puzzled, and it is unfortunate that there is no record of what he thought. Did he pity the fanaticism of Jews who would fight for an empty room? Did some sense of awe or wonder come over him? Did he have even the slightest glimmering that here was an idea which within four centuries would dominate his world? Or, and this must be the most likely, was his attitude just that of an inquisitive tourist looking at the wonders of the east? Pompey turned on his heel and walked out; he did no damage to the Temple and left its Treasury intact.

The Romans set up a new dynasty, the Herodians, to govern Judaea, and they were definitely client-kings. Although they were members of the Jewish faith, the Herodians were far from strictly orthodox. Their leading personality, Herod the Great, who reigned 37-4 B.C., was a cruel, ambitious man of considerable ability. He built a new administrative capital, Caesarea, on the coast and equipped it with temples for Roman worship. He built a chain of fortresses to protect his eastern frontiers, among them the rock stronghold of Masada on a precipice above the Dead Sea. Above all he set about rebuilding the Temple to make it the biggest and most splendid place of worship in the world. Much of the revenue for this would have come from the numerous Jewish communities outside Palestine, of whom Herod attempted to stand in some sense as protector; it is unlikely that Herod's motives were primarily religious—he probably thought more in terms of attracting pilgrims, pacifying his own subjects and of the erection of a splendid building as an end in itself. Characteristically, he erected a golden eagle, symbol of Rome, over the building and this of course caused uproar among religious Jews who hated all graven images.

The most probable date for the birth of Jesus of Nazareth is some time in the last years of Herod the Great, who died in

4 B.C. (Perhaps the point should be cleared up at this stage that the modern calendar, dating years from before and after the birth of Jesus, was devised by a miscalculating Greek monk in the sixth century A.D.)

Herod the Great's son proved to be an ineffective ruler of Judaea and in A.D. 6 the Romans deposed him and took the province under the direct rule of Prefects appointed from their army. The most famous of the Prefects, Pontius Pilate, ruled from A.D. 27 to 36, and he ordered the execution of Jesus of Nazareth. Religious Jews had disliked Herod the Great and they could stand the Romans no better. The country was in continual ferment and potential rebellion, much of it aroused by the hope of a miraculous leader, the Christ, who would deliver them ('Christ' means 'anointed one'; it was the Greek version of the Hebrew word 'Messiah'). Neither the effects of Jesus of Nazareth nor subsequent Jewish history can be assessed without taking into account the way in which many Jews were obsessed by the thought of miraculous intervention by Yahweh. (But the idea of Yahweh himself appearing in human form occurs in no known Jewish tradition; the Christ, like the prophets of old, would be a human being equipped with divine authority.) As a people the religious Jews were in a strange, even unique condition of national expectancy; at any moment the world was about to be transformed by intervention by Yahweh. Every political difference with the occupying power had religious overtones and every political problem was in part religious. From the Roman point of view, the Jews in Palestine were the most difficult people in the whole empire. The fact that the Jews did not agree even among themselves and that the more conservative or Hellenised of them did not believe in the coming of the Christ merely added to the tumult.

The pot boiled over in A.D. 66, about thirty years after the crucifixion of Jesus, when Messianic Jews rose in outright rebellion. It was partly a fight for independence from Rome and partly a civil war. One leading personality, Josephus, rebel governor of Galilee, changed sides to the Romans; he later wrote his history of the Jews which is the leading source for the period. The fighting lasted seven years and was by far the most difficult outbreak of its kind that the Romans had ever encountered. The difficulty was the fanaticism of the rebels against enormously superior forces; they believed that they only had to keep going for the Christ to appear to save them. (Actually the idea of the Christ being a military leader had not previously been prominent in Jewish tradition; he had been thought of primarily as a just ruler and judge.) Up to the very last moment as the Roman besiegers broke into Jerusalem (A.D. 70) the defenders expected the Christ to come, but instead most of them were massacred and the Temple was burned down, never to rise again.

After the fall of Jerusalem, the last of the rebels held out for three years more in the fortress of Masada, still hoping for the Christ. But in steady siege operations Roman legions of 30,000 men built a great ramp up the cliff for the final assault. No Christ had appeared and on the night of April 15, A.D. 73, the leader, Eleazer ben Ya'ir, called together the 976 inhabitants of the garrison, men, women and children. Lots were drawn to select ten men to kill everyone else. Then the ten drew lots for one to execute the remaining nine. Finally the last man committed suicide. When the Romans stormed the fortress they found the whole community dead. (Two women, however, hid and escaped and told the story.) Recent archaeological research has uncovered what may be the actual fragments of pottery used for the drawing of the lots.

Even this disaster did not break the nationalist Jews. There followed a period in which the Romans seem to have made some attempt at conciliation but it ended in A.D. 132 when the Emperor Hadrian proposed to build a temple to Jupiter on the site of the former Jewish Temple in Jerusalem. An aged rabbi, Akiba, was at the centre of resistance and he proclaimed its military leader, Simon bar-Cochbar as the Christ. (The name bar-Cochbar, meaning 'son of the Star', is itself of religious significance; a star was one of the heavenly signs associated with the Christ and was given a place in the Matthew version of the Jesus birth story.) This time it took the Romans two years to crush the rebellion and afterwards they took steps which, successfully, destroyed Judaism as a political force. Jerusalem was made a forbidden city for Jews and many of them left the Holy Land altogether.

Of course Roman military success did not end the Jewish religion. Cut off from its main territorial roots, and with its Temple destroyed, it became an entirely spiritual faith with the synagogues as its organisation and the scholarship of its rabbis as its support. By the end of the second century A.D. it was turning in upon itself and ceasing to be a proselytising religion; this, presumably, was partly due to Christianity being more popular to converts and partly to the loss of prestige involved in military defeats and the non-appearance of the Messiah. Nevertheless it evolved into a system capable of commanding the adherence of many generations, often under conditions of persecution. In the eighth century A.D. the prophet Mahomet used a combination of Jewish-Christian traditions and his own insights to found the religion of Islam: his followers, like the Christians, acknowledged the invisible God of the Jewish scriptures. From time to time new expectations of the Christ arose among the Jewish communities and the tradition of the occasional appearance of a 'miraculous rabbi' continued into the twentieth century. In present day Jerusalem there flourish ultra-orthodox Jewish groups which cause embarrassment to the State of Israel because they repudiate its authority; they say they prefer to await the Christ.

Jesus of Nazareth was a product of this religion when it was in full flood of youthful vitality and just approaching a turning point in its history.

---

[1] Is 40: 15–28
[2] Is 40: 10–11; 30–31
[3] Is 45: 21–24; 66: 23–24
[4] Ps 39: 5–10
[5] Jer 11: 13
[6] Ps 139: 1–3
[7] Ps 137: 1–6
[8] Is 61: 5–6

II

The Training of a Religious Genius

A TENDENCY has existed, particularly in the late Protestant tradition of Christianity, to portray Jesus of Nazareth as a sort of hick preacher from the backwoods who by honest simplicity could outsmart the college professors. Such sentimental verses as 'There is a green hill far away' have formed a part of this rustic picture. Thus to dismiss someone who arguably was the most influential man who has ever lived is to do less than justice to him. Jesus was a tense, intelligent person with convictions formed from studying a sophisticated, complicated religion of which he lived at the centre; he mastered his material and put it over with a sharp turn of wit. He must have possessed a strong, even hypnotic personality. He had a gift for healing. There was nothing 'far away' about the country in which he lived. It was a rich populous land which in its geographical situation between Europe, Asia and Africa stood at the heart of world civilisation. People who preach simplicity are not necessarily themselves of simple intellect: Prince Gautama, the Buddha, was certainly a man of sophisticated upbringing and so, in our own century, was Mahatma Gandhi. In attaching moral importance to simplicity, Jesus is more likely to have chosen to do so through exercise of a lively intellect rather than through mere instinct.

The mainstream Christian tradition is that Jesus started his public teaching at around the age of thirty and was executed after three years at most but possibly after only one year. Indeed taking into account his periods of withdrawal, his actual public teaching may have lasted only a matter of weeks. The briefness of his work is in strange contrast to the normal methods by which prominent personalities have, over a long period of years, built up their reputations. Jesus was by any worldly standard an ephemeral figure.

Almost no tradition—except apochryphal ones full of miracles—exists about the nature of Jesus's life before he started teaching, but the matter of his upbringing and early experiences cannot be ignored. They must have been significant to his formed personality. It is simply not sufficient to write off most of his life by sentimentalising him as a carpenter thinking up great truths while labouring in his workshop: even the gospels, taken literally, make no such claim. When he returned to Nazareth and started preaching it seems to have been after an absence and people had to exercise their memories to recall that he was the carpenter's son. The carpenter theory is inherently improbable because it is not the way that great ideas can be expected to come. Moreover, Jesus's teachings reflect a sophisticated knowledge of the Jewish thought of his day and this must have come from careful, intelligent study. Jesus was an accomplished theologian. The only gospel story about his childhood is that as a boy of twelve he gave his parents the slip and went to argue with wise men at the Temple. This may have ritualistic rather than biographical significance but it is not incredible to suppose that some such incident took place. One can readily imagine the rabbis being amused and interested at the remarks of a child who appeared to be a religious prodigy and trying him out to see how much he knew.

The lack of evidence about Jesus's life has led to extravagant legends. There is a tall story to the effect that he visited Britain and studied the Druids, who had a sophisticated religion. Another legend sends him to Tibet which was then not yet Buddhist but a place of sorcerers and spells. If he had really wanted to, Jesus could have gone to either place; there was a regular shipping service to Britain for the tin trade and, with difficulty, he could have made his way towards Tibet on the caravan routes. But such stories must be written off because there is not the least indication in Jesus's teachings that they had taken place. His teaching was entirely Jewish in content. If he did travel at all, the most probable journey would have been to Egypt which was an important centre of Jewish life and thought. It was in Egypt that Jesus's contemporary, the Jewish philosopher Philo, was trying to work out a synthesis of Judaism and Hellenism, arguing that revelation and reason should be mutually interdependent. While Philo's writings were to be of considerable value to early Christian thinkers they were remote from Jesus's own mode of thought, which concentrated on the Jewish side of things.

What can be known for certain about Jesus's early life?

The name 'Jesus' is simply the Greek version of the Jewish name 'Joshua' which means 'Help of Yahweh' or 'Yahweh is Help'. It was a common name of the time and can be allowed no special significance save that it hints possibly at religious parents. It might be compared with the modern name 'Mary' as given to a girl; 'Mary' may indicate, but not necessarily, devout Roman Catholic parents. That Jesus's home was a devout one can be guessed at from the fact that it seems to have produced not one but two sons who exerted wide religious influence: that is Jesus himself and his brother James, the later leader of the Jerusalem Christians. The gospels, however, indicate some family hostility to Jesus's preaching activities.

The question of Jesus's surname is more difficult. Of course 'Christ' is not a surname at all and it is incorrect to use it as such: as has been mentioned it means 'the anointed one' and is the Greek equivalent of the Jewish title 'the Messiah'. If used at all to denote Jesus, the title should be given the definite article, 'the Christ'. Jesus was not referred to as 'the Christ' during his lifetime. According to the Jewish custom of the time, Jesus would have been surnamed after his father, or after his home town or after his trade; there might well have been a flexible usage by which at various times he was called after all three. His father's name, by unanimous tradition, was Joseph and so the most obvious way of naming Jesus is to call him Jesus ben-Joseph (ben = son of). This was a thoroughly routine Jewish name of the period, almost in the category 'Jack Jones' or 'Bill Smith' in a modern English-speaking country. He is more identifiable to the modern reader if he is called 'Jesus of Nazareth' after his home town and that is the usage adopted for this book; 'Nazareth' does, however, arouse incidental problems which are dealt with later. The third possibility is 'Jesus the Carpenter' or 'Jesus, Son of Carpentry'. ('Son of' was used to denote a man's trade as well as his parentage.) While unanimous tradition is to the effect that Jesus was brought up in the carpentering trade by Joseph, the word 'carpenter' could, conceivably, have some mystical significance. The Hebrew word for carpenter can, in its written form, have a possible alternative meaning of 'sorcerer': so the possibility cannot be totally excluded that there is more to the carpentry tradition than meets the eye.

The tradition that Jesus belonged to the 'House of David' and so was of royal blood is of ritualistic significance only. King David had been dead for about 1,000 years in the time of Jesus and his royal line had ceased to be distinguishable. Quite possibly Jesus was a descendant of David but only in the sense that the greater part of the population of modern Britain can safely number William the Conquerer among its forebears. 'Son of David' was one of the titles of the Jewish Christ and anybody who claimed to be the Christ would, automatically, claim also Davidic descent. In practical Jewish politics of the time, Davidic descent in itself was not a factor and nobody claimed a special position on the strength of it.

All in all, it can reasonably be assumed that Jesus belonged to an undistinguished family of non-priestly status and that he would have been brought up in some trade or craft, for which carpentry is the most likely candidate. There was nothing abnormal about such a background producing a distinguished religious teacher; many of the leading rabbis were of exactly similar background—the famous Hillel, for example, was originally a shoemaker from Babylon. It was a normal Jewish custom to teach every boy a trade. Rabbis were supposed to be self-supporting from their own work. Such a trade as carpentry is useful anywhere and during periods of religious study Jesus could have earned a living by doing such odd jobs as were available; this would have been as normal as a modern university student taking paid work in his vacations. While there is no evidence of exceptional poverty in Jesus's background, his circumstances appear to have been humble. He belonged to the skilled working class.

Evidence about the size and attitude of his family is conflicting. Joseph appears to have died by the time he had started teaching and there is some evidence of hostility from the mother and brothers; conceivably it was felt he should be working to support the family instead of engaging in so much religious activity. But the accounts are inexplicit and little significance can be attached to them; it is not clear whether the term 'brother' includes cousins. At least one brother, James, appears to have been very devout and became a leading personality among Jesus's followers after the crucifixion. His mother, too, seems ultimately to have joined the Jesus group. The first ten bishops of Jerusalem were reckoned to be blood relations of Jesus and this suggests the existence of a family clan, which would be quite a normal thing.

The most single significant fact about Jesus's background is that according to unanimous tradition he was a Galilean. That is he belonged to the northern province of Palestine. Many consequences flow from this and, indeed, much of his life is incomprehensible unless his Galilean background is borne constantly in mind.

So far as twentieth century comparisons are possible and not pressed too far, Galilee stood to the Jewish heartland of Judah in something of the same kind of relationship as New York stands to Washington or Birmingham stands to London. Galilee was a rich, cosmopolitan province with its own king, who was subject to the Roman Legate of Syria. The main communications routes crossed it and the population tended to be of mixed blood; Jesus himself may well have belonged to a mongrel family background. There were Jews, Egyptians, Greeks, what now would be called Arabs, Persians, people from Mesopotamia and, probably, a few negro Africans all jostling together in a densely populated area. The population was probably around two million, half of it Jewish. The capital, Sepphoris, was a largely Greek city to the west of Lake Tiberias (the 'Sea of Galilee'). The Jewish population of Galilee, many of whom had entered the faith by intermarriage or conversion, were regarded with suspicion or even scorn by the orthodox hierarchy in Jerusalem. Because of their continual contacts with non-Jews it was difficult for them to keep ritually clean and many Galilean Jews were lax in religious observance. At the other extreme, some Galilean Jews reacted by becoming exceptionally devout and militant. The hills of Galilee were the haunt of the Zealots, a highly religious group which sought to help along the cause of Yahweh by armed force against people who did not share their tenets. In Jesus's boyhood they rose in major revolt under a Christ-like leader called Judas of Galilee.

Jesus's home town is stated by the gospels to be Nazareth, which stands today as a rather ugly town on a hillside near Lake Tiberias. It is the main Arab centre in the State of Israel and has a strong Communist Party. Conceivably, there may be some esoteric significance in attaching Jesus to it. The earliest Christians were called 'Nazarenes' and there is some possibility that a 'Nazarene' sect of ascetic Jews existed before Jesus: the word means 'holy ones' and has no necessary connection with the town of Nazareth. Jesus's brother, James, is stated to have been a member of this sect and to be bound by its vows. Was Jesus also a member of the Nazarenes and did Christianity evolve from this group rather than from just him personally? The question is an obscure one and there is insufficient evidence to go into it. But to be ultra-safe about the historical Jesus it is best to describe him as a Galilean without laying too much stress upon the town of Nazareth, especially as there is no independent evidence that the town even existed in his day. (Many Galilean towns are mentioned in contemporary, or near-contemporary, documents but not Nazareth; of course it may well have just been too small to be worth mentioning.)

The Galilee region is one of singular beauty, with glorious vistas from the mountain sides and with Lake Tiberias running up the middle. Modern agricultural methods, inaugurated by Jewish Zionists and imitated by native Arabs, have restored it to much of the wealth and fertility it had in Jesus's day. In summer, the plains can get unpleasantly hot but it is always possible to ascend to the cool highlands. To walk in Galilee or sit by Lake Tiberias on the calm of a Sabbath is an experience both stimulating and restorative; it seems to be the perfect setting for the teaching of eternal truths, a place for clarity and for opening the soul. It is so exactly the right context for Jesus that one almost expects to meet him around the next hairpin bend as one drives down to Tiberias. But there is danger in over-sentimentalising this aptness. Galilee in Jesus's time was a busy, cosmopolitan area and not primarily a place for dreams. No doubt so intelligent a man as Jesus would have derived some benefit from communing with nature in beautiful Galilee and this would have had some influence upon him. However, there was much more to Jesus than appreciation of scenery.

Given that he was the child of devout, orthodox Jewish parents, his first education would have been in the local synagogue under its rabbi. The synagogue was a lay institution and the rabbi, who was then supposed to support himself by his own trade, was a layman. So far as a rabbi was 'ordained' it was by his learning being recognised by other rabbis in the school of thought to which he belonged. Any Jewish teacher might be called 'rabbi' informally, as a title of respect, and apparently Jesus was, although there is no evidence of his being officially qualified. The synagogue was a place of worship, a place of argument (anybody could get up and interpret the sacred texts, provided his views were not too outrageous), and a place for instructing children.

Jesus's native language was Aramaic, a popular form of Hebrew. He would have learned it with the peculiar Galilean accent which was sing-song and scorned by the socially-conscious in Jerusalem. At the synagogue he would have learned to read and write classical Hebrew as a pre-liminary to the detailed study of the Jewish scriptures. In addition, he probably picked up colloquial Greek, which was the lingua franca of the Roman Empire and the daily language of many communities in the Galilee region. His dialogues with Pontius Pilate and with other Roman officials would have been in Greek. It is highly improbable that he learned Latin. His formal education was in Judaism, not in the Greek and Roman classics.

At this period the party of the Pharisees had acquired more or less complete control over the synagogal system and there is ample evidence in Jesus's teachings that he had had a Pharisaic upbringing. Indeed in at least the broad sense of the word Jesus remained a Pharisee all his life; during his teaching period his disputes with other Pharisees were about peripheral matters only and had nothing to do with basic Pharisaical doctrines on God, on man and on the relationship between God and man. In particular, he took the Pharisaic view that the dead, or at least the righteous dead, would be resurrected on the coming of the Christ.

The Pharisees are possibly the most fruitful sect which has ever existed: they are the direct ancestors of both Christianity and modern Judaism. Their origins are obscure and stretched back three or four centuries before Jesus, or even back to the Babylonian exile. They had emerged into the full light of history during the Hasmonean period, about a century before Jesus, and were now at their full flood of vigour. They were a broad party, with room for different colours of opinion, but the principle Pharasaical concepts, common to them all, are distinctive.

They preached Judaism as a universal religious faith and not just the political cult of a particular tribe. They were vigorous missionaries and largely or wholly responsible for the expansion of Jewish membership that was taking place. In their view a man became a Jew not so much by birth as by circumcision (usually accompanied by a ritual ceremony of washing) and remained a Jew by obeying the dietary and ritualistic requirements of the Torah—the Jewish way of living. They spent much of their energy on what they called 'fencing' the Torah, that is defining and strengthening its basic precepts and adapting them to new conditions: this was a considerable work of philosophy and scholarship to which many of their best minds devoted their lives. To the outsider the Torah can look like a wearisome, even superstitious, burden of detailed rules and in Christianity, after Jesus's time, there grew up some tendency to denigrate the Torah and to say that Jesus had brought a new message which liberated men from wearisome obligations. In fact, of course, the earliest of Jesus's followers continued to observe the Torah and Jesus himself enjoined obedience to it. To the Pharisees the Torah was not a burden to be endured but a joy to be savoured—the joy of living in the way Yahweh had directed.

The Pharisees had brought into Judaism elements which exist either faintly or not at all in the Old Testament; they believed that they had an oral tradition which was as valid as the written documents. Thus the Old Testament says almost nothing about life after death but the Pharisees taught a doctrine of the resurrection of the dead which would happen when the Christ came. Details varied but the underlying doctrine was that good Jews would not, through death, be obliged to miss the great day of the Christ; they would be brought back to life to share in the good times. Some teachers extended the doctrine to cover the resurrection of all men; the non-Jews or the bad ones would be brought back to life for the purpose of being punished. What happened to people in the interval between death and resurrection was none too clear; there was a vague idea of souls dwelling in 'Sheol', a shadowy underworld, but no systematic teachings. The idea of a 'soul' existing independently of the body has never been congenial to mainstream Jewish thought. There was, however, some idea of praying for the welfare of the dead. Details varied between different teachers and different sets of traditions and the common link was a belief in at least some kind of resurrection of the dead at the appearance of the Christ. This, of course, was Jesus's teaching also and he was as vague as the Pharisees about the details; it took the Christians three or four centuries to work out a complete system of heaven, hell, purgatory and resurrection, although today they are tending to return to the primitive vagueness.

Then the Pharisees believed in the existence of multitudes of invisible beings; there were angels, who were messengers and assistants of Yahweh, and there were demons who were evil spirits who went around doing harm. Some Pharisees went to considerable lengths to work out the names and hierarchies of these beings; they formed, in some sense, the Jewish equivalent of the multitudes of deities which existed in popular Hellenism. Jesus's life, as portrayed in the Christian gospels, is incomprehensible unless this background is taken into account. Alien as it may seem to many people of the twentieth century, Jesus, by every indication, took for granted the Pharisaical doctrines on spirits. His was a world thronged with invisible beings. This tradition long continued: John Henry Newman as a young Anglican clergyman in the

1820s taught that angels were in immediate control of everything that happened in the world.

During Jesus's boyhood the leading Pharisees were divided
into two main schools, those of the rabbis Shammai and Hillel
who taught regularly in Jerusalem and attracted multitudes
of disciples. Their teaching was a sort of dialectic, much of it
being in question and answer form; teacher and disciples
combined to set out doctrine. Anyone could attend these
'schools' and the influence of them spread rapidly through
Judaism, rabbis carrying the doctrines to the most distant
synagogues: the whole teaching was based, of course, on a
thorough mastery of the Jewish scriptures and was incomprehensible apart from them. Shammai and Hillel concerned
themselves mainly with questions of conduct and morality
and with the 'fencing' of the Torah. There was some rivalry
between them, or between their adherents, but on most
matters of substance they were in agreement. Their dif-
ferences might be likened to those between Jesuits and
Dominicans in the modern Roman Catholic Church. Without delving into detail, it can be reckoned that Shammai was
the more interested in the technicalities of the Torah while
Hillel concentrated more on the spirit behind it. Asked to
summarise the Torah, Hillel, in a famous phrase, said: 'Do
not unto others that which is hateful to you; this is the whole
law.' These words were spoken in around the year A.D. 10
when Jesus was still in his boyhood. The attitude of Hillel was
to be significant both in later Judaism and in Christianity and
Jesus himself obviously leaned towards the school of Hillel
rather than that of Shammai. Whether this came about
through teaching from a Hillel-type rabbi in his home
synagogue during his formative years or whether he picked
it up later does not particularly matter; what is clear is that
Hillel must have been an influence upon Jesus and a familiar
figure to him. As a boy, Jesus may well have heard Hillel
teach.

Most of the smaller Jewish sects were offshoots of the great

Pharisee party. While the mainstream Pharisees held a generalised belief in the coming of the Christ, and to a greater or lesser extent scanned the scriptures to try to predict when he would come, they had time to think of other things as well. The tendency within the sects was to regard the arrival of the Christ as imminent and all-important, the only thing that really mattered.

In Jesus's home country of Galilee there was the prominent sect of the Zealots of which he must have had knowledge and with which he may well have had some kind of association. In Judaism, as in later Christianity and Islam, there existed some tendency to help along the work of the Lord by armed force and the Zealots exemplified this; they advocated active resistance to unholy government and were particularly keen on assassinating fellow Jews whom they believed to be collaborating with the enemy. However, the Zealots were not just a secular resistance movement but also a religious sect with their own doctrines derived by their own teachers from the scriptures and, probably, from direct inspiration. They looked to the imminent coming of the Christ. Exactly what Jesus's relationship was with this group is none too clear but it may be a reasonable deduction that some of his later teaching was directed against it. The bias of Jesus was towards awaiting the Christ and meanwhile avoiding violence: his epigram 'All who draw the sword will die by the sword'[1] appears to be entirely his own and to be aimed against Zealot-type activities. (Of course mainstream Pharisees were also distrustful of the Zealots.)

Thus the net result of considering Jesus's early background is to produce a devout young Galilean, speaking with an accent, thoroughly imbued with a Pharisaical outlook, probably with a bias towards the school of Hillel. He had a detailed knowledge of the Jewish scriptures and probably had been made to learn long sections of them by heart.

In the world of Jerusalem, to the south, Jesus would have appeared as something of a provincial. But he would have known Jerusalem well, and presumably, like every devout Jew, would have loved it above all places on earth.

Jerusalem, built on a hill, remains to this day a stirring city. The best method of approaching it is from the east in late afternoon. One is literally going 'up' to Jerusalem. The city is built largely of the local yellowish bricks, as it presumably was in Jesus's time, and the traveller gets his first glimpse of it high above him, the sun shining on it to give it a golden glow. 'Jerusalem the golden' has a literal as well as a symbolic meaning. There is no natural reason for Jerusalem's existence; it stands on no ancient communications routes and has no industrial or agricultural advantages. It is a place built for religion and because of religion; its origins stretch back to the earliest period of Judaism and it may well have had religious significance even before that. The main ancient site within it was a piece of bare rock in the Temple on which, it was said, the patriarch Abraham had agreed to sacrifice his son, Isaac, at Yahweh's behest; this story of a father sacrificing his son played an important part in Jewish theology and was much discussed in Jesus's time. The point of it was that Isaac, although saved at the last moment, was a willing victim: it was held that his willingness had in some sense 'redeemed' the Jewish people. The rock was held also to be the foundation stone of the world.

In Jesus's time Jerusalem was busier and more spectacular even than it is today. It was the centre of the widespread Jewish faith and every devout Jew made at least one pilgrimage to Jerusalem during his lifetime. Such a Galilean of devout background as Jesus might well have come annually from childhood onwards. There were literally hundreds of synagogues representing different schools of teaching and different nationalities and languages. It was a wealthy place from the annual 'Temple tribute' arriving from Jews all over the known world and from the expenditures of the pilgrims. It was said that as many as a million Jews were known to attend the Passover festival in Jerusalem and while this must have been an exaggeration the numbers must certainly have run into many tens of thousands. The city was a Lourdes and Mecca rolled into one. The modern State of Israel has, for sentimental reasons, made Jerusalem into its capital but it keeps its crucial Department of Defence at the main centre of population, the coastal city of Tel Aviv. In Jesus's time there was no idea at all of Jerusalem being a political capital. The capital of the prefecture of Judah, in which Jerusalem lay, was Caesarea, the largely non-Jewish city built by Herod the Great on the coast. It was at Caesarea that the Roman Prefect lived with his main garrison. Jerusalem was the religious centre of the Jews and the Prefect would visit it with a view to maintaining order during the major festivals.

The dominating feature of Jerusalem was the enormous Temple which had been erected by Herod the Great and was being finally completed during Jesus's boyhood. Twice the area of St. Paul's Cathedral, London, it was probably the biggest place of worship in the world and it was certainly world famous. Unfortunately there is no record of its actual architectural style but it was definitely a rich and awe-inspiring building. The inner section, the Holy Place, was sheathed in sheets of gold and from its hilltop situation the sun could be seen flashing upon it for many miles around. The first glimpse the approaching pilgrim got of Jerusalem was the Temple. About thirty years after the execution of Jesus, the Temple was to be destroyed but the Jews cherished the memory of it and wrote down detailed accounts of it. While these accounts may to some extent be an idealised version they can at least in outline be taken as trustworthy.

All Jerusalem lived in the shadow of the Temple. It was difficult to sleep through the dawn for the sound of the silver trumpets heralding the first sacrifice of the morning. The trumpets continued to sound at intervals during the day and it was said that they were so loud that they drowned all conversation in the city. The Temple was served by 20,000 hereditary priests—their families still survive under the

name of 'Cohen'; of these about fifty were on duty on any
particular day. (Most of the priests lived by their own trades
and were called for Temple service only once or twice in
their lifetimes: the qualification, besides birth, was an un-
blemished Jewish background and a form of ordination or
admission to the priesthood.) Under the priests served an
hereditary caste of Levites who looked after the lesser details
of the administration of the Temple and provided huge
choirs, hundreds strong. At the head of this powerful
organisation stood the High Priest who, formally, was the
top man in the Jewish faith: the Hasmonean rulers had
combined political authority with the religious functions of
High Priest. At the time of Jesus, the High Priest was chosen
from a narrow circle of inter-related families and the
appointment was either made directly by the Roman Prefect
or had to be confirmed by him. The Prefect held the High
Priest's ceremonial vestments in his own custody and handed
them out when they were required for high festivals. It was
a delicate balance of power which gave the Romans some
influence over the Jewish ritual but less than complete control; it depended upon restraint from both sides. The Temple
authorities, while obviously repudiating Roman religious
rites and the disposition to deify the Emperor, did conduct
sacrifices to Yahweh on Caesar's behalf.

From the point of view of the outsider the Temple was a
mysterious, awesome place, the home of a weird but powerful
superstition. Synagogue services were difficult enough to
understand; the way the Jews lifted up and revered scrolls of
the scriptures looked as if they were worshipping pieces of
writing. The Temple was a gigantic shrine with, apparently,
no god inside it. By a custom which had developed during the
previous two centuries the Jews had ceased even to pronounce
the name 'Yahweh', regarding it as too sacred. Instead they
used such circumlocutions as 'the Lord', 'Adoniai' or the
'Holy One' when the name occurred during the reading of
the scriptures, and this made their religion yet the more

mysterious. From the outsider's point of view, all that could be deduced was that this anonymous, invisible deity was capable of commanding widespread allegiance.

About half the Temple area consisted of the open-air Court of the Gentiles, which anyone could enter. Apart from a big carving of a grape-vine, there was no emblem from which the outsider could guess at the nature of the Jewish God. The Court of the Gentiles was a busy place containing stalls at which traders sold animals for sacrifice. There were also money-changers' stalls—the Temple had its own special currency. It was also something of a religious Hyde Park Corner, with rabbis of various persuasions discussing theological details and preaching to the world at large. According to the New Testament both Jesus himself and, after his execution, his first followers, taught in the Temple and sought to attract converts there. It appears that anyone who belonged to the Jewish tradition was free to propound his views; in case of disorder there existed a special force of Temple police and a Temple prison. Beyond any reasonable doubt, Jesus from youth upwards must have been familiar with the Court of the Gentiles and the rabbis who taught there; as his knowledge grew, he must have joined in the debates and discussions. He appears, also, to have become impatient with the commercial activity going on around, the cries of the stallholders and money-changers being an unpleasant distraction from the discussion of the more sublime and subtle facets of religion.

From the Court of the Gentiles, members of the Jewish faith could pass into the Court of Women. From this a wide, semi-circular staircase led upwards to the smaller Court of Israel. Only male Jews who had been circumcised were allowed to ascend these steps and fragments are still extant of a notice, in red, which in Hebrew, Greek and Latin threatened death to any non-Jew who went up them. The severity of the penalty indicates the Jewish concern with ritual cleanliness and, also, the existence of a definite threat from outsiders. It was said, for example, that the Samaritans went out of their way to pollute the inner Temple by smuggling in rats. (The Samaritans, a semi-Jewish group, had their own community and their own temple in Samaria, which lay to the west of Jesus's own province of Galilee.) The Court of Israel was partly a place in which to say prayers and partly a waiting area where men lined up before taking their sacrificial animals into the Court of the Priests beyond. The central feature of the Court of the Priests was the Altar of Sacrifice which had something of the air of a butcher's shop, with all day long animals being slaughtered and offered to Yahweh. Some of the sacrifices were communal ones offered on behalf of the whole Jewish faith; others were offered for private purposes—it was usual for the devout Jew to appear from time to time at the Temple, purchase an animal and offer it to the priests for sacrifice for purposes connected with his own life.

Behind the Altar of Sacrifice stood the towering Holy Place, the only covered part of the Temple. The outer section of it contained sacred emblems of the Jewish faith, notably the seven-branched candlestick and the Altar of Incense. Then came the inmost shrine, the Holy of Holies, veiled off by a curtain and entered only by the High Priest and by him only once a year, on the Day of Atonement. The Holy of Holies was an empty, unlit room, the supreme symbol of the Jewish invisible God.

It is now 1,900 years since the Jewish Temple was destroyed but it is still possible to recapture some of the excitement and tension of the Temple rites. The Day of Atonement was the occasion upon which the Chosen People, the Jews, with prayer and fasting affirmed their relationship with the ultimate powers of the universe. They believed they were the uniquely privileged people of the Lord and possessed of a truth which was more powerful than anything else in existence. The gods of Rome had secured political mastery of the world but beside the Jewish invisible God they were worthless. Moreover the relationship between the Jews and their God was not just a static one; the Jews believed that this invisible force intervened actively in the affairs of men and at any moment might overturn the existing world order by sending the Christ. On the Day of Atonement the whole Jewish people fasted and prayed and thought of what was happening in the centre of their faith, Jerusalem. At the climax of the Temple ceremonies, the High Priest, in his vestments, walked away from his attendant priests and acolytes and, a solitary figure, stepped into the Holy of Holies. There he claimed the supreme privilege of addressing the Lord face to face, by his proper name. It was the only time the sacred name was ever spoken and the High Priest did so in a whisper—'Yahweh'.

The other great festival of the year was the Passover, which celebrated the Lord's power to deliver the Jews from their enemies. It was in part a family feast, conducted in the home by the head of the household in the form of a ceremonial supper. This, of course, still continues in Judaism as the Seder meal and had already become traditional by the time of Jesus. But it was also an integral part of the Temple rites and tens of thousands of pilgrims arrived every year to celebrate the Passover in Jerusalem. The supper took place on a Sabbath evening (that is a Friday evening, the Sabbath being reckoned from dusk to dusk) and the preceding afternoon the heads of family lined up at the Temple with their paschal lambs, which the priests slaughtered. A bit of the fat of each lamb was offered on the altar but the rest of it was taken home for the family Seder meal. The rule was that no bone of the paschal lamb might be broken. While the slaughter in the Temple was going on, the choir of Levites sang Psalms 113–118 '. . . He raises the poor from the dust; he lifts the needy from the dunghill to give them a place with princes . . .'[2]

The Christian gospels give the moment of Jesus's death as that at which the annual paschal lambs were being slaughtered in the Temple.

The controlling authorities of the Temple, including the High Priest and his associates, belonged to a kind of Jew which has not yet been considered. They were of the Sadducee party. This was a conservative group under aristocratic leadership which had emerged during the Hasmonean period about a century earlier. Unfortunately the Sadducees are now known only by the accounts of their opponents so it is difficult to be definite about them. Since, however, both Christians and mainstream Judaism have blamed them for Jesus's execution, it is necessary to look at them.

The distinguishing mark of the Sadducees was a lack of religious 'enthusiasm' and a cautious attitude towards doctrine. The Sadducees held rigidly to the Pentateuch but they were doubtful about the later prophets and repudiated altogether the Pharisaical claim to possess an oral tradition as valid as that of the scriptures. They rejected the Pharisees' doctrine of the resurrection of the dead, believing it to be an unauthorised novelty or, even, a superstition. They attached little or no importance to the doctrine of the Christ being sent by Yahweh to deliver the Jewish people; it was the kind of teaching which stirred up the people and so did more harm than good. Perhaps the Sadducees were akin to the Erastian fox-hunting clergy of the eighteenth century Church of England; they deplored religious excesses, adopted many of the customs of the secular society around them (in the case of the Sadducees this meant Hellenist-Roman society) and believed worship should be restricted to a proper time and place. Although the Sadducee party is usually reckoned to have been upper class in composition, it would appear probable that a good many ordinary Jews in practice followed its ways. The Pharisees, on the other hand, were the evangelical party whipping up the people in the synagogues towards a more lively and more total view of religion.

Jesus could argue with Pharisees but with the Sadducees he could have no intellectual contact at all. Both socially and

theologically the Sadducees represented a conservatism
which was alien to his way of thought. As a convinced
believer in the doctrines of the Christ and of the resurrection
of the dead, Jesus found the Sadducees outside his terms of
reference. Conversely, the Sadducees had no respect for any
provincial prophet from Galilee; debate and argument about
the finer points of theology were not to their taste.

The mainstream Pharisees supported the Temple and
doubtless numbered many of the priests among their party;
they saw it as the central symbol of the Jewish faith. Nevertheless their teachings and the forms of home and synagogue
worship they fostered were creating a new form of Judaism
within the shell of the old. The destruction of the Temple in
A.D. 70 meant not the end of Judaism but the victory of the
Pharisee spirit, now freed from material encumbrances. The
Sadducees disappeared. The memory of the Temple remained fresh and to this day the reputed remnant of it, the
Western Wall (nicknamed the 'Wailing Wall'), is still a prime
object of Jewish pilgrimage; nevertheless, practical Judaism
for 1,900 years has flourished on the basis of home and
synagogue only. When Zionist Jews in the mid-twentieth
century recovered control of Jerusalem they had no serious
proposal for building a new Temple and the prevailing view
among the ultra-orthodox appears to be that such a venture
should await the coming of the Christ.

Jesus's attitude towards the Temple appears to have been
much the same as that of the mainstream Pharisees. He may
well, like them, have had some reservations on the manner in
which it was conducted, but he certainly accepted it as an
institution. In his recorded teachings there is no evidence of
him encouraging his followers to neglect their Temple duties.
Moreover the Temple continued to exist for a full generation
after Jesus's execution and during that time the early Jerusalem Christians went on performing Temple duties and,
presumably, offering animals for sacrifice. In the long run,
however, the Christians were to prove as adept as the senior

heirs, the Jews, at maintaining a religion without the Temple.

That Jesus did not repudiate the Temple is a point of some substance. Some Jewish sects of his time, and ones which contained teaching at many points close to his and that of the early Christians, *did* repudiate the Temple. They believed that the Temple had been polluted by the corrupt Sadducee priesthood and that it was following an incorrect calendar; until the Christ arrived to put things right, the faithful should keep away from it. Moreover they taught the existence of a 'new covenant', that is a new treaty between Yahweh and the elect which superseded that made, according to Jewish tradition, in the time of Moses.

This type of Judaism, which in many respects is similar to Christianity, was at its peak at the time of Jesus but its full significance was not realised until the discovery of the scrolls from the Dead Sea in the present generation. The scrolls, found from 1948 onwards in caves to the north of the Dead Sea, were the library of a Jewish sect. When they were first discovered there was some controversy about their date but now it is generally agreed that they pre-date the fall of the Temple in A.D. 70 and so can be regarded as almost exactly contemporary with Jesus. Their value is two-fold. In the first place they include the oldest known copies of the Hebrew scriptures and so are of high interest in checking the authenticity of the modern text; they show that, on the whole, the scriptures of the Old Testament have been handed down with a high degree of accuracy. In the second place they give an account of the teachings and the way of life of a Jewish sect which, plainly, was a direct forebear, and possibly the parent, of Christianity. The deciphering and analysis of the scrolls is as yet far from complete but ample is already known to show that they profoundly modify former historical concepts.

Jesus must have known about the Dead Sea sect and its teachings. This could, possibly, have been only at second-hand but the overwhelming probability must be that he, as an intelligent young man deeply interested in religion, must have visited it himself and spent time there. It was a power-house of radical Jewish thought.

The sect's headquarters, Qumran, lies less than a day's walk from Jerusalem. The Dead Sea surroundings are parched and inhospitable; they are the lowest dry land on earth. If the fruitful beauties of Galilee may have given Jesus an instinct for the bounties of Yahweh, the austerities of the Dead Sea hint at the rigours of Yahweh. Living as in a kind of oven, the sectarians gave their lives to prayer and to the study of religion. In Jesus's time they had existed for about 200 years, that is as about as long as the Methodist Church has existed today.

Recent excavations have uncovered the actual buildings used by the sect and today tourists clamber over them. They appear much more realistic as the birthplace of Christianity than the garish shrine at Bethlehem fifteen miles away; there are ritual baths, a communal dining room and a scriptorium for copying out the sacred texts, and it does not require too excessive an exercise of the imagination to envisage the young Jesus of Nazareth studying among them.

Almost certainly the Qumran sect was identical with the Essenes, a group whose existence has always been known from the writings of Josephus, Pliny and Tacitus. Qumran, it can be taken, was their central community but groups of them were also dispersed across Palestine, usually living on the edges of Jewish towns and villages.

The Essenes, on the basis of the Dead Sea scrolls, were a group of priests and laymen who had repudiated the Temple and the whole existing Jewish establishment. Their original leader had been an unnamed 'Teacher of Righteousness' who in around 150 B.C. had been murdered by a wicked priest in Jerusalem. They now looked forward to the appearance of two Christs, one a priest and the other a king, an event they believed to be imminent. They thought of the universe as the scene of a cosmic battle between darkness and light. They held their property in common, attached high value to celibacy and lived a monastic or quasi-monastic form of life. They believed in the resurrection of the dead. Initiation into the sect was by baptism, accompanied by the taking of oaths, and to replace the Temple rituals they had a ceremonial meal, with the presiding priest blessing bread and wine. They wore white robes. They were interested in astrology and possibly also in some form of sorcery or communication with the dead, although the latter point is as yet far from proved, and presupposes the startling idea that they were willing to run counter to the definite injunctions of the Book of Deuteronomy. While the inner doctrines and rituals of the sect were reserved to the initiated, they did undertake some public preaching activities and, also, healed the sick. (Preaching and healing were intertwined activities in the Judaism of this period and are difficult to consider separately.) Their methods of healing were presumably based in part upon scientific knowledge, that is the application of drugs and herbs, and in part upon prayer or faith healing. It is possible that the actual word 'Essene' means 'healer': the alternative derivation is 'holy one'.

An extreme view is that the Essenes actually invented Christianity and the person of Jesus for purposes of their own, not yet fully understood. So startling a proposition requires, however, much more proof than has so far been produced. A safer view is that Jesus and the early Christians were profoundly influenced by them and, indeed, could hardly have existed without the Essene groundwork but that in the last analysis Jesus was an independent teacher with doctrines of his own. Jesus to the Essenes was something like Martin Luther to the Roman Catholics.

In matters of ritual the similarities are almost uncannily close. For example, there is the ritual meal. In mainstream Judaism, ritual meals were and are part of the routine of religious practice; the custom in Jesus's time was to bless bread at the beginning of the meal and wine at the end of it. The Essenes, however, blessed bread and wine together with no interval and this has passed into Christian practice. (Actually the New Testament is contradictory on the point. Accounts of the Last Supper in Matthew and Mark have Jesus blessing bread and wine without an interval: Luke and Paul's first letter to the Corinthians, have the wine blessed after supper. The gospel of John does not mention the matter at all. Overwhelmingly, Christian rites have been based on the Matthew and Mark procedure and this, of course, is Essene.) Then the Essene ritual meal was restricted to initiates in good standing and the Christians have followed a similar practice; in mainstream Judaism, on the other hand, any guest may join in a ritual meal. The question of eating the body and drinking the blood of the Christ, in the form of bread and wine, did not arise in Essenism. However, the Essenes did regard the meal as a substitute for Temple sacrifices and the worshipper consumed bread and wine in place of a sacrificial animal; this, too, passed into Christianity once the doctrine had been developed of Jesus as 'the lamb of God'.

In phraseology and turn of thought the Essene and Christian scriptures are sometimes so close to each other as to lead to the certain conclusion that the first Christian writers had been soaked in Essene lore. No other explanation is possible. Yet the Christians seem to have added their own twist to the Essene teachings and not to have taken them over uncritically. This can plainly be seen in the most frequently quoted example of coincidence of the two sets of scriptures.

In the gospel of Matthew, Jesus is reported as saying: 'I was hungry and you gave me food; I was thirsty and you gave me drink; I was a stranger and you made me welcome; naked and you clothed me, sick and you visited me, in prison and you came to see me.'[3]

In the Testaments of the Twelve Patriarchs, a book used by the Essenes and of which fragments have been found in the Dead Sea caves, the following words occur: 'I was beset with hunger, and the Lord himself nourished me. I was alone and God comforted me: I was sick and the Lord visited me: I was in prison, and my Lord showed favour to me.'

Obviously either Jesus himself or the writer of Matthew, or both, must have had the Essene phrases echoing in their minds, although it cannot be known whether the imitation was conscious or unconscious. Equally obviously the similarity is in phrasing only, not in meaning. The Christian passage refers to the dealings of man with the Christ; the Essene passage is the other way round and refers to God's dealings with man.

Then there is the question of celibacy. Jesus of Nazareth by every account was an unmarried man and celibacy has always been prominent in Christianity (although Jesus, according to his reported teachings, did not lay any stress upon it.) In mainstream Judaism, in Jesus's time as well as at every other time, celibacy has never been regarded as a virtue; indeed one of the tests of a good rabbi in the Jewish tradition is that he should be the head of a well-ordered family. That Jesus was a celibate rabbi would make him stand out as an oddity, as living, in Jewish terms, an incomplete life. The Essenes, however, did practise celibacy and thought that sex polluted a man. So in this respect Jesus must be classified as belonging to the Essene rather than the mainstream Jewish tradition and the tendency continued among at least some of the early Christians.

How numerous the Essenes were is impossible to establish but there were probably several thousands of them and because of their distinctive way of life they were a well-known group. They regarded themselves as the inner citadel of Judaism and had an introspective outlook; their secret doctrines were suitable only for the initiated who were bound by oaths of obedience. They believed in reserve and privacy and made no attempt to evangelise the multitudes. An Essene recruit was a man deeply interested in religion who of his own volition came humbly to the order and requested instruction: most of the members, probably, had been trained in the lore since childhood. However, it was almost inevitable that such a group would contain rebels who would rebel against the restrictions and seek to make the Essene doctrines more widely known. Such a man seems to have been John the Baptist who can be taken to have become a prominent public teacher at the time when Jesus was in his twenties.

It is a fair deduction that John the Baptist had been a member of the Essene order and that from his way of life he still regarded himself as bound by Essene vows. He left the discipline of the brotherhood to proclaim to the world at large the doctrine of the imminent coming of the Christ, doubtless in a simplified way suitable for the multitudes. He urged the people to repent their sins and lead moral lives and had no hesitation about the criticising the official Jewish leadership. He gave his converts a ritual washing, or baptism, to fit them for the coming Kingdom of Heaven but instead of joining the disciplined Essene order they continued their ordinary lives as laymen. The traditional site at the River Jordan where John baptized his converts is only three miles from Qumran. He must have been a powerful, persuasive preacher and the scraps of evidence that exist about him suggest that his followers continued as a distinctive group after his death: the early Christians were at some pains to claim that they were John's legitimate heirs.

Jesus must have known about John and heard him preach; indeed the gospels state that Jesus and John were blood cousins and had known each other since childhood. The gospels state that Jesus was baptized by John and that the ceremony marked the start of his public teaching. Whatever the details of the influence of the two men on each other, Jesus certainly adopted the same line as John of simplifying the inner doctrines of advanced Judaism and preaching them to the Jewish masses. It may well be that John was a decisive influence in Jesus's life. In terms of public repute, John appears to have been a far more powerful figure than Jesus was in his lifetime: John's teaching probably continued for a longer period of time and his followers were more numerous. The contemporary Jewish writer Josephus thought it necessary to describe John and his followers as part of the Jewish scene of the time but gives no mention of Jesus's ministry.

All the influences upon the young Jesus so far described — the Pharisees, the Temple, the Qumran Essenes and John the Baptist — were all readily accessible to his home. It would have required no unusual effort for him to have learned from them. But did he, possibly, travel a little further afield? He could, for example, have gone to Damascus where there existed a strong Jewish sect, which may or may not have been Essene and which preached its own lore on the coming of the Christ. Damascus was a journey of only a day or two from his Galilean homeland. Then, with a little more difficulty, he might have travelled to Egypt where, in the desert, existed the interesting sect of the Therapeutae who were an offshoot of the Essenes and included both men and women. While it cannot be asserted with absolute certainty that they were in existence as early as the time of Jesus, they did belong to the same general climate of ideas as early Christianity. The most striking thing about them is that they seem to have taken the ritual meal a stage further than the Essenes and to have given it a sacramental character. Their scriptures refer to the 'blessed bread of life and . . . the blessed cup of immortality' as if they were technical terms. There must, surely, have been some interrelationship between them and the early Christians and the possibility cannot be excluded of Jesus himself having contact with them.

The broad conclusion to be drawn of the whole of Jesus's background is that he lived in an atmosphere of the liveliest religious controversy and debate. People were going to extremes in interpreting the Jewish scriptures and traditions. It was a time of wonders, dominated by the belief that God was about to send the Christ and so transform the world.

Questions of conduct and belief were of paramount importance as the radical Judaism, to which Jesus belonged, boiled
up towards the great revolts against Rome. Jesus knew
exactly what was going on and knew his way around the
tangle of scripture, interpretation and prophecy. Also he was
a Galilean and he remained a Galilean, a radical remote from
the Temple 'establishment'. Jews of his kind believed that
revolution was imminent and when Jesus started to preach
his keynote was: 'The time has come and the kingdom of God
is close at hand.'[4]

[1] Mt 26:52   [3] Mt 25:35-36
[2] Ps 113:7-8   [4] Mk 1:15

III

The Propagandist

THE decisive characteristic of Jesus of Nazareth is that he was a brilliant propagandist. Neither theologically nor morally was there much that was particularly novel in his teaching; most of it already existed in the Judaism of his time. The point of Jesus was that he could simplify and present doctrine in a way that could give it a mass appeal without making it so trivial as to insult the intellect. His impact upon his own generation was slight but for many generations after his own time some of the best minds found stimulation in his words, as recorded, and so did multitudes of the simple. While the narrative sections of the gospels are difficult to analyse because they were written for ritualistic rather than historical purposes, many of the actual words of Jesus, as reported, do bear the mark of having been spoken by a real person with a tense personality. There is reason to suppose that the first three gospels, the synoptics, are based upon authentic traditions of the sayings of Jesus and that the fourth gospel, that of John, although primarily theological, does enshrine an additional, supplementary tradition.

Of course it is hopeless to look for a scholarly agreement about what is historical and what is ritualistic in the gospels. They are among the most difficult documents known to man and there is no consensus of opinion upon them. What matters is that if they are read through at a sitting, and taken as a whole, they do, in the experience of many, give a vivid picture of a real person. Such an impression is the more vivid if they are read in a translation which puts them into everyday language: the King James Authorised Version, for example, should be avoided — despite its literary qualities it is inaccurate in content and now so archaic in tone as to fog up the story.

Jesus emerges, firstly, as a man convinced that he has a special relationship with the divine. He speaks with authority. This, of course, was well within the Jewish tradition of the inspired prophet. He is a young man but not an immature one; he has mastered the complexities of the Jewish religion and he has had some experience of the working of the world. He has a strong personality and gifts of healing. He is the kind of person that gets talked about. He is highly intelligent, has a quick wit and knows a lot about practical psychology.

What were his methods?

The most characteristic thing about him is his indirect teaching and use of parables. This was not unique and may be related to the contemporary Jewish sectarian habit of concealing secret doctrines in a code. Indeed in Matthew's gospel Jesus is specifically stated to have said that he concealed his doctrines in parables so that outsiders would not understand them. But whatever was his actual intention, the effect of most of the parables is to put into memorable and simple form the most complex teachings about theology and morality. An anecdote is always more memorable than a statement of fact: a good deal of twentieth century journalism and advertising is based upon this proposition. Jesus's parables are brilliantly formed. They are close to real life and include a surprise twist which jerks the reader's mind. Nobody has ever made up such good parables as did Jesus and so, if for this reason alone, he can be regarded as one of the world masters of propaganda.

A good example of his technique, at its most brilliant, is the parable of the prodigal son. The story is of a man with two sons, the younger of whom claims his share of the family estate and goes away and squanders it on extravagant living. The elder son remains respectably at home. When the younger one runs out of money, he returns to his father with a modest request to be allowed to work as a hired servant. The father, to the annoyance of the elder brother, regards the prodigal's return as an occasion for rejoicing and gives a feast to welcome him. There is no moral lesson in this, no advice on how people *ought* to behave; it is, rather, an astute and convincing description of how people often *do* behave. The story arrests attention because it is such an interesting sidelight on human behaviour and by applying it to the dealings of God with man, Jesus presents God as an attractive and understandable figure. Another parable, on similar lines, is that of a shepherd who has ninety-nine of his sheep safely penned up but one of them missing; it is the missing one that he worries about. Again this is recognisable human behaviour and so an attractive way of describing God. The parable of the labourers in the vineyard goes a little beyond customary human behaviour. It tells of a man who hires labourers to work for a day in his vineyard for an agreed wage. Later he hires more labourers for only half the day. All, at the end, get the same wages irrespective of how long they have worked. Applied to the dealings of God with man, it is a memorable, even shocking, illustration of Jesus's doctrine of divine mercy.

Jesus also used parables to teach direct moral lessons of how people ought to behave. The most memorable in this category is the story of the good Samaritan. It tells of a traveller on the road between Jerusalem and Jericho (a road which, incidentally, ran near to the Essene headquarters at Qumran) who gets beaten up and robbed. A priest sees him lying half dead on the roadside but passes by on the other side without helping him. A Levite does the same thing. Then along comes a Samaritan who takes pity on him, binds up his wounds and pays for him to be accommodated at an inn. The story must have had the greater impact because of the ill-feeling which existed between Jews and Samaritans at that time; the very phrase the '*good* Samaritan' would have sounded to many Jews like a contradiction in terms. It is a fair supposition that this parable, retold through the centuries, must have been the direct cause of a good many acts of human generosity which otherwise would not have taken place.

In addition to his parables, Jesus used vivid imagery and similies, particularly in relation to his doctrine of a forthcoming 'Kingdom of Heaven'. They pour out in profusion, some sections of the teachings, as recorded, consisting of a torrent of continuous, ever-changing metaphor. The effect is compelling. Thus in the thirteenth chapter of Matthew, the Kingdom of Heaven is likened successively to a man sowing seeds, to a harvest, to a mustard seed growing into a tree, to yeast, to treasure hidden in a field, to a merchant selling everything to raise funds to buy a fine pearl and to a fisherman's net. Few professional poets have been so successful with their imagery as was Jesus. Some of the most powerful imagery is that referring to God, whom Jesus presents variously as a shepherd, as a father, as a wealthy philanthropist and as a generous employer; the implication throughout is that the supreme force in the universe can be understood in human terms and should be regarded with mixed awe and affection. The 'father' metaphor, which was one of Jesus's favourites, is a particularly compelling one, fitted to human psychological need. Of course, it was not Jesus's invention—the concept of God as a 'father' was a part of ordinary Judaism—but in his constant use of it Jesus made it characteristically his own. It remains to the present day as one of the leading doctrines of Christianity.

Then there are Jesus's epigrams and witticisms, struck off on the spur of the moment to fit particular situations. He appears to have been a brilliant, if disconcerting, conversationalist and a difficult man to defeat in verbal argument. Like all such people, he was good at switching the ground of argument to that which suited him best. Sometimes he parried a question by asking a question himself. Sometimes he used paradox: 'Anyone who wants to save his life will lose it; but anyone who loses his life for my sake will find it. What,

then, will a man gain if he wins the whole world and ruins
his life? Or what has a man to offer in exchange for his life?'[1]
Questioned by one lot of Jewish officials about his authority,
Jesus refuses to answer; instead he poses the conundrum of
whether they think John the Baptist's activities were
divinely inspired, which was difficult for them to cope with
in public on the spur of the moment. To grapple with him
verbally was like trying to clasp quicksilver. Asked whether
Jews should pay tribute to Rome, he called for a coin and
asked whose head was portrayed on it. The answer came:
'Caesar's.' So Jesus said: 'Very well, give back to Caesar
what belongs to Caesar—and to God what belongs to God.'[2]
This, of course, was only a verbal trick, which settled
nothing, but it appears to have done its task of the moment
of confusing his opponents.

Allied to his powers as a verbal propagandist were Jesus's
powers as a healer and miracle worker. Of course it is hopeless to try to analyse the miracles in the manner of a modern
psychic researcher. Also it is hopeless to try to find 'natural'
explanations of them. In the late nineteenth and early
twentieth centuries attempts were made to portray a non-
miraculous Jesus, an entirely rational teacher who was
endowed with special powers by the imagination of his
followers. This tendency is not entirely extinct in that many
Christian preachers still talk as if the gospel reports of Jesus's
words are somehow more reliable than the reports of his
actions. In fact words and miracles were part and parcel of
the same thing. Right into the present century, stories of
miracles have cropped up from time to time in Christianity,
in Judaism and in all other religions. In Jesus's own time,
Galilee appears to have been a particularly fruitful source of
wonder-working rabbis. Even Jesus's alleged power of being
able to heal while a long distance from his patient was not
unique to him.

The authenticity or otherwise of Jesus's miracles is now
impossible to judge. The modern reaction to a supposed

supernatural event is generally one of the utmost scepticism. For example, the Roman Catholic authorities carry out the most exhaustive medical tests before allowing the authenticity of any miraculous cure at Lourdes; the official reaction to a Lourdes miracle appears to be one of suspicion rather than joy. In Jesus's time reactions were entirely different; a miracle was an object of awe rather than of suspicion. Had people not believed Jesus to be a miracle worker, he would be unlikely to have attracted a following in the short time at his disposal. And it is not unreasonable to suppose that Jesus possessed some special skill or gift in healing illness. Such things do arise quite often. The nature of the control of the mind over the physical processes of the body is as yet not understood, although it is clear that such things as skin disease often have mental origins. Like a modern faith healer or Christian Science practitioner or, even, like a modern general practitioner administering a placebo, Jesus could sometimes cure illness by getting at the patient's mind. To this day, the Roman Catholic anointing of the gravely ill ('extreme unction') is held to have a medicinal as well as spiritual purpose. The overwhelming probability must be that if the gospel accounts of Jesus are even remotely accurate, then he was widely regarded as a worker of supernatural wonders and there must have been some basis for this reputation.

The puzzle must be how so talented, scintillating and persuasive a personality emerged apparently so suddenly. A man's opinions may change at a particular moment of time but his skills are usually with him for all his mature life. The gospel accounts, with their strongly ritualistic overtones, do not seriously deal with this point. One possible explanation of it is that at some stage in early manhood Jesus realised that he possessed exceptional powers but decided not to exercise them until he had completed a prolonged course of study and formed his opinions. Then, at a moment deliberately chosen, he began to exercise them publicly in the established tradition of the wonder-working preachers of Galilee. Such an explanation is credible if Jesus is allowed the extreme, but not impossible, degree of self-control that is necessary for it. But on this type of question it is dangerous to dogmatise or be too precise. Jesus was not a significant figure to the world at large in his own lifetime; there is no mention of him in contemporary Jewish or Roman documents. He acquired a staggering significance only after his death. Men who were not trained historians and who were in a condition of emotional excitement then looked back to him and to the shreds of tradition that existed about him; it is unlikely that they were photographically accurate in portraying him and such large areas of his life are missing from the records altogether that we cannot know for certain that he emerged only suddenly. The true explanation may be some factor now lost and unguessable.

Strangely enough, Jesus's actual words and actions, although apparently they were so striking, were of relatively little interest to the first generation of his followers. What mattered was the status given him as the Christ and the prospect of his early return armed with plenipotentiary divine powers. For example, Paul of Tarsus wrote plentifully about Jesus but nowhere in his words, as voluminously preserved in the New Testament, is there any discussion of Jesus's parables, epigrams and miracles: so far as Paul was concerned, the parables of the prodigal son and the good Samaritan might never have been told at all. It was only after Jesus had failed to return that, as a kind of substitute, his followers began to pay close attention to what he had said. Then Jesus the propagandist came into his own and a new religion was founded in part upon what he had said.

But did Jesus really intend to found a new religion? Is it possible at this distance of time, with so much of the evidence missing, to establish with any degree of certainty what his true motives were? The next chapter attempts to answer these questions.

¹ Mt 16:25–26   ² Mt 22:21

IV

The Ideas of Jesus

THE theme which runs right through Jesus's teachings was of a cosmic revolution which was about to upset the existing order of nature. 'The time has come and the kingdom of God is close at hand,'[1] he said. God was about to intervene in the affairs of the world in a most dramatic and unmistakable way. The dead would be brought back to life and the Christ, an inspired leader with miraculous powers, would be the ruler. All injustices would be set right, the wicked would be punished and the righteous would be rewarded.

Torn out of its context, such teaching looks like the words of a fanatic or an eccentric. But in the Jewish society of the time, there was nothing abnormal about it. Many religious Jews believed that they were living in, literally, the last days of the existing world order and that enormous miracles were about to take place. The Qumran community, for one, based its whole existence upon this proposition. The dead were often buried in clothes suitable for wearing when they came back to life in the resurrection — an event believed to be imminent. As the Jews boiled up towards the great revolt of A.D. 66, they became obsessed with the doctrine of the coming of the Christ and many leaders, teachers and scholars put forward their ideas about it. The ordinary people, especially in Galilee, were swept by waves of fervour. From the distance of the twentieth century, such an atmosphere may appear uncongenial or absurd but what matters is that it existed. To preach about a coming cosmic revolution was no more unusual in first century Palestine than to debate about the finer points of Marxist theory in twentieth century Milan.

It requires fine scholarship to distinguish precisely how Jesus's doctrine of the kingdom of God differed from that of other contemporary teachers and since the raw material is deficient such scholarship cannot arrive at final conclusions. But one point that does stand out in Jesus, and was to be of considerable importance for the future, is that he talked of the kingdom of God as being not just a cosmic revolution but also a revolution in men's hearts. 'The kingdom of heaven is within you,'[2] he said. This, of course, did not exclude imminent pyrotechnics from the sky—'I tell you solemnly, before this generation has passed away all these things will have taken place'[3]—but was supplementary to them. When the Christ did fail to appear in glory, Jesus's followers were able to fall back upon the interior 'kingdom' inside men's hearts and with the passing of time it became more and more important; in the twentieth century it stands as the leading doctrine of mainstream Christianity.

From the inadequate, and contradictory evidence available, it is difficult to get behind Jesus's words to his actual intentions. Did he, for example, have any idea at all of founding a new world religion which would last for many centuries? The answer is probably in the negative. He was so concerned with the imminent cosmic revolution that it would not have occurred to him that anything in the nature of the Christian Church was necessary. There is, of course, the text in Matthew in which he is quoted as giving the nickname 'rock' to his disciple, Peter, and saying 'Upon this rock I will build my church.'[4] Some scholars consider this to be a later interpolation and not based upon Jesus's own teaching at all: be that as it may, it is beyond doubt that the words are uncharacteristic of Jesus's sayings as a whole and are not part of any settled line of teaching.

Anyway, in practice the Christian Church has not claimed its title deeds from Jesus's public teaching. It has based itself upon a mystical Jesus in heaven and upon inspiration from God after Jesus's death.

Jesus confined his teachings almost entirely to Jews. There was no necessity for him to have done this. Palestine, and especially Galilee, in his time had a mixed population and had he wanted to, Jesus could easily have broadened his appeal: perhaps about half the population was non-Jewish. So far as is recorded, Jesus ignored for teaching purposes such centres as Caesarea, capital of Judaea, and Sepphoris, capital of Galilee; they were cities of Greek culture and so did not contain devout Jews. There was nothing unusual in a sectarian Jewish teacher making such a limited appeal; it was difficult enough to get the chosen people on the right lines without worrying about outsiders. In fact Jesus is specifically quoted in the gospels on the undesirability of casting pearls before swine; that is putting divine truths before people incapable of understanding them. Thus he was in a sense much narrower in outlook than many of the Pharisees of his time who thought it was a positive duty to convert non-Jews and carried out successful missionary work to this end. It might be objected that Jesus's teachings were cut short by his early arrest and execution and that if he had been allowed to live a normal span and to teach for forty-five years, as the Buddha did, he would have broadened his appeal. This, of course, is unknowable but Jesus's teachings were so soaked in the Jewish scriptures and in the inner refinements of Jewish thought that he would have had to have adapted them to make them comprehensible to outsiders. The universalist elements in his teachings are buried within the Jewish context. Provided the analogy is not carried too far, his methods can be likened to those of such a modern Christian revivalist as Dr. Billy Graham, who normally takes for granted in his audience at least some knowledge of the Euro-American idea of God.

Jesus's moral teachings, although brilliantly expressed, contain little that was new. His most vivid moral idea, that one should love one's neighbour as oneself, was already fundamental in Judaism. (He was quoting an injunction directly from the Book of Leviticus.) Indeed on most of the basic moral questions the major religious teachers of mankind have been agreed: the difficulty has been less to set out a code of human conduct than to get people to follow it. In moral, as opposed to theological, matters, Jesus and the Buddha would have found themselves largely in agreement. Jesus, like the Buddha, insisted that thoughts were as important as actions and that it was possible to sin without physically doing anything; the same idea appears in the Jewish ten commandments—'You shall not covet your neighbour's house. You shall not covet your neighbour's wife, or his servant, man or woman, or his ox, or his donkey, or anything that is his.'[5] On moral questions Jesus is important more for his eloquence than for his originality.

Like all, or almost all, the influential thinkers of mankind, Jesus insists that happiness cannot be attained through merely material means. He put over this idea above all else in the series of statements known as 'the sermon on the mount'. The opening passage is a partly liturgical speech, soaked from beginning to end in Jewish lore, and concluding with the simple sevenfold petition known as the 'Lord's Prayer'. Full analysis of the whole sermon would require a book in itself but it is worth quoting, with references, to give an idea of how it was formed.

'How happy are the poor in spirit;
theirs is the kingdom of heaven.'[6]

(This apparently obscure statement has some reference to the Essenes, who renounced possessions and preached the value of poverty. Both the Essenes and the early Christians sometimes called themselves 'the poor': lack of possessions was equated allegorically with a humble outlook towards God.)

'Happy the gentle:
they shall have the earth for their heritage.'[7]

(This is a direct allusion to Psalm 37: 'The humble shall have the land for their own to enjoy untroubled peace':[8] 'gentle' and 'lowly' are alternative translations.)

> 'Happy those who mourn:
> they shall be comforted.'[9]

(This reflects Psalm 126: 'Those who went sowing in tears now sing as they reap,'[10] and Isaiah: 'Yahweh has anointed me . . . to comfort all those who mourn.')[11]

> 'Happy those who hunger and thirst for what is right:
> They shall be satisfied.'[12]

(This is the same doctrine as the Book of Proverbs: 'He who pursues virtue and kindness shall find life and honour too,'[13] and follows the imagery of Psalm 42: 'As a doe longs for running streams, so longs my soul for you, my God.')[14]

> 'Happy the merciful:
> they shall have mercy shown to them.'[15]

(Apart, possibly, from a reference in the Book of Samuel to David being merciful to Saul, this can be taken to be original; it is in the same vein as Jesus's parable of the master who forgave his servant a debt.)

> 'Happy the pure in heart:
> they shall see God.'[16]

(This is a straightforward adaptation of Psalm 24: 'Who has the right to climb the mountain of Yahweh, who the right to stand in his holy place? He whose hands are clean, whose heart is pure . . .')[17]

> 'Happy the peacemakers:
> they shall be called sons of God.'[18]

(Several Old Testament writers praise peaceable men but none in exactly this way. Jesus's use of 'sons of God' is interesting here as illustrating how the terms was used in his time; obviously 'son of God' in this sense did not imply divinity.)

> 'Happy those who are persecuted in the cause of right: theirs is the kingdom of heaven.'[19]

(No direct parallel in the Old Testament but in keeping with the Essene spirit.)

Most modern preachers illustrate their sermons with quotations from the scriptures. This opening passage of the sermon on the mount goes a stage further than that; most of the preacher's words are actual scriptural quotations. When he wants to say something, he looks into the scriptures for a formula to express it. Obviously to be able to do this the preacher must have his mind soaked in scriptural knowledge and his audience, too, is probably capable of recognising the allusions. The whole passage is an early Christian ritual formula, probably learned by heart and repeated as a kind of incantation. Conceivably Jesus put it like this to help people to learn it; or, more probably, some later hand put together traditional sayings of Jesus into this form.

The sermon on the mount goes on to affirm Jewish traditions. 'Do not imagine that I have come to abolish the Law or the Prophets. I have come not to abolish but to complete them. I tell you solemnly, till heaven and earth disappear, not one dot, not one little stroke, shall disappear from the Law until its purpose is fulfilled.'[20] This sounds like a real Jesus, not a fictional person, insisting with all the emphasis at his command upon his doctrine.

Then comes a section which, as the Dead Sea scrolls show, is closely related to Essene doctrine. Both Jesus and his audience must have had the Essenes in mind. Part of this section is in agreement with the Essenes and the rest of it explicitly indicates Jesus disagreeing with them.

Thus the statements: 'Anybody who is angry with his brother shall answer for it,'[21] 'If a man looks lustfully at a woman he has already committed adultery with her in his heart',[22] 'Do not swear'[23] and 'Offer the wicked man no resistance',[24] are all paralleled in the Essene documents and Jesus is endorsing them.

Then comes the most startling piece of doctrine in the whole of Jesus's preaching and one that is his alone, with no exact parallel in any other religion.

'You have learnt how it was said: You must love your neighbour and hate your enemy. But I say this to you: love your enemies and pray for those who persecute you.'[25]

Until the discovery of the Dead Sea scrolls, the first of these sentences had no apparent meaning. Nowhere in normative Judaism or in the Old Testament is there any injunction to 'hate your enemy'. But the Essenes of Qumran did think, in a mystical sense, that it was their duty to do so. Their documents contain such injunctions as 'to hate all the sons of darkness' and to bear 'an eternal hatred toward all men of destruction'. The initiation oath included a pledge to love fellow members of the order and to hate its enemies. So this appears to be the source from which Jesus's audience had been instructed to 'love your neighbour and hate your enemy'. In telling his audience to love their enemies Jesus was contradicting Essene teachings which were well known. It would be interesting to know exactly how the Essenes put out this teaching; could it, for example, have emerged in the sermons of John the Baptist?

The injunction to 'love your enemies' is superhumanly difficult, if one thinks about it seriously, and only a minority of Jesus's followers have ever obeyed it. It implies not just an intellectual regard for one's enemies' best interests but also an emotional feeling of affection for them. While it is closely similar to the teachings of the Buddha, who taught reverence and love for all living things, it is, in the form Jesus put it, unique. Judaism, too, while preaching a doctrine of just conduct towards all men, contains no commandment to *love* one's enemies. Was the commandment sheer unworldliness on Jesus's part, unrelated to the real life of men, or in an increasingly dangerous world could it yet come to seem more practical than any alternative?

Jesus's extraordinary vehemence breaks through in passages which have worried commentators ever since. 'If your right eye should cause you to sin, tear it out and throw it away; for it will do you less harm to lose one part of you than to have your whole body thrown into hell. And if your right hand should cause you to sin, cut it off and throw it away; for it will do you less harm to lose one part of you than to have your whole body go to hell.'[26] Was this a considered statement by Jesus, intended to be taken literally? Certainly some Christians have followed it literally and it has led to cases of self-mutilation. The third century theologian Origen, for example, castrated himself so as to get rid of sexual temptation. The more common interpretation, however, is that Jesus was speaking allegorically and trying to make his hatred of sin as vivid as possible. On this reasoning, the 'tear it out and throw it away' passage must be counted as propaganda rather than doctrine. A crucial point about it is that it is so strange that it sounds like an accurate memory of what Jesus actually said—there is no apparent motive for a later writer to have made it up—and so it gives an unusually reliable clue to the kind of person Jesus was. He was a tense, excited visionary labouring under an extreme sense of urgency. He burned with enthusiasm to get men to behave well against the imminent coming of Christ; like many geniuses, he lived at the limit of sanity—it is unreasonable to expect a genius to be a balanced man.

In the form given in the gospels, the sermon on the mount is not a balanced, systematic treatise. Anybody who attempted to adopt it as his sole rule of conduct would rapidly find himself in difficulties. Parts of it are humanly impossible to obey and other parts are ambiguous or difficult to understand. Probably, indeed, it originally was not a single sermon at all but was a set of various sayings, attributed to Jesus, which the gospel writers strung together to make a continuous passage. Nevertheless, its imagery and force are capable of making a profound impression. The ideas thrown off by this remote, oriental preacher, in a white heat of enthusiasm about a coming cosmic revolution, must count, historically, as among the most influential things ever spoken. The sermon on the mount must be regarded as the work of an artist rather than an architect; it paints in the most vivid highlights but provides no detailed plan.

Jesus's extreme tension, exemplified in the sermon on the mount, sets him apart from many other major figures of world religious history. At the opposite pole from him is the calm figure of the Chinese Confucius, who advocated balance and a respect for tradition; the aim should be to produce what he called 'the superior man', who controlled his passions and lived to a high ethical standard. 'The superior man makes honesty the foundation of existence,' said Confucius. 'He uses it with address and consideration. He speaks of it with modesty and carries it out with sincerity and faithfulness.' The Buddha, too, is a much calmer figure than Jesus, although on moral matters his teaching and Jesus's boil down to much the same thing. (Interestingly, even the miracles attributed to the Buddha have a similarity to those attributed to Jesus, including a multiplication of food to feed disciples.) On the whole, the Buddha preached a doctrine of cause and effect, of bad actions leading to bad results; the concept of punishment from the wrath of a personal God was alien to him. 'The fool does evil deeds while unaware of what they lead to. By his own deeds the stupid man is burned, as though burned up by fire. The fools, unwise, behave as if they were their own worst enemies, committing many evil deeds which issue then in bitter fruits. Nor is an action called "well-done", which makes us suffer afterwards, of which we reap the fruit in tears, with weeping, wailing and lament. That action only is "well-done", which brings no suffering in its train, of which we reap the fruit quite glad, in happiness, with joyous heart ... An evil deed need not at once cause trouble to the man who did it. It keeps up with the careless fool just as a fire, smouldering under ashes ... The iron itself creates the rust, which slowly is bound to consume it. The evil-doer by his own deeds is led to a life full of suffering.'

The fourth Sikh Guru, Amar Das (1552–74) laid down the rule: 'If anyone treat you ill, bear it. If you bear it three times, God himself will fight for you the fourth time.'

The visionary prophet Mahomet, despite his sense of contact with the divine, sets out the earthiest doctrine of all with a direct appeal to standard human emotions and full recognition of sexual pleasure. 'O men! ye are but paupers in need of God; but God is the Rich, the Praiseworthy! If He pleases, He could sweep you away, and bring forth a new creation ... Verily they who recite the Book of God, and observe prayer, and give alms in public and in private from what we have bestowed upon them, may hope for a merchandise that shall not perish ... We have made the Book a heritage to those of our servants whom we have chosen. Some of them injure themselves by evil deeds; others keep the midway between good and evil; and others, by the permission of God, outstrip in goodness; this is the great merit! Into the gardens of Eden they shall enter: with bracelets of gold and pearl shall they be decked therein, and therein shall their raiment be of silk ... But for infidels is the fire of hell; to die shall never be decreed to them, nor shall aught of its torment be made light.'

Throughout the gospels, Jesus is portrayed as scoring off the 'Pharisees' in argument and the impression might well be gained that part of his purpose was to do down Pharisaical teachings and replace them with his own. Actually the term 'Pharisees', as used in the gospels, is too vague to be meaningful. The Pharisees of Jesus's time were not a single disciplined party but adherents of a broad school of thought which had room for many sub-divisions. They stressed the spiritual side of the Jewish religion and devoted much attention to fostering the Jewish way of life, with its rules on diet and ritual purity. Most of them were pious, learned men and their authority

6

was growing; it was from them that modern Judaism sprang. In Jesus's time they had already acquired a large measure of control over the synagogue system and were the religious teachers best known to the people. Jesus himself was Pharasaical in his general outlook and his disputes with individual Pharisees that he encountered were about peripheral matters. While for reasons of their own, the writers of the gospels are obviously anxious to stress the points of divergence (the gospels having been written at a time when Christianity and Judaism were separating into two religions), even they do not suggest that the Pharisees as an organised party had anything to do with the execution of Jesus. Persecution of people for their beliefs has never been a characteristic of Pharisaical Judaism. Jesus, according to the gospels, was executed by the Roman Prefect, abetted by the Jewish High Priest, who belonged to the party of the Sadducees, who were unsympathetic to the Pharisees.

In all advanced religions there exists an inevitable tension between the 'letter' and the 'spirit', that is between people who think formal rules at all costs should be preserved and people who think that the philosophy behind the rules is more important. Such tension can plainly be seen in modern Christianity, in Islam and in Buddhism and it certainly existed in the Pharisaical Judaism of Jesus's time. Successful practitioners lean to one side or the other but are careful to keep a balance, and this is what Jesus did. The rival Pharasaical schools of Hillel and Shammai, which had grown up during Jesus's boyhood reflected the two tendencies, Hillel leaning towards the 'spirit' and Shammai leaning towards the 'letter'. Neither of them went to an extreme and nor did Jesus. While definitely a 'spirit' man, Jesus certainly did not repudiate the letter of the Jewish Torah. 'The scribes and Pharisees', he is quoted as saying, 'occupy the chair of Moses. You must therefore do what they tell you and listen to what they say; but do not be guided by what they do; since they do not practise what they preach.'[27] A good many mainstream

Pharisees of the same period shared this view precisely as, indeed, do most modern Christian preachers. It would be an injudicious vicar who proclaimed from his pulpit: 'Imitate me!' (The scribes were a form of lawyers who gave official interpretations of the Jewish Torah; they were mostly members of the Pharisaical party and need not for present purposes be distinguished from it.)

All the encounters between Jesus and the Pharisees described in the gospels show Jesus coming off best in argument. Whether or not there were also arguments in which Jesus was worsted is not stated; obviously it would be human for tradition to enshrine the Master's successes rather than his failures. But even the gospel writers do not present the Pharisees in totally bad light. The Pharisees are shown treating Jesus with courtesy and putting legitimate questions to him about his teaching. Judaism is a religion of debate and, particularly in this period, there was nothing unusual in a prophet claiming a special inspiration and being challenged in argument. Indeed without this atmosphere of debate, Jesus could hardly have existed at all; it is difficult to imagine a modern prophet, claiming a direct line to God overriding other authority, being allowed to preach in St. Peter's, Rome, or the Methodist Central Hall, as Jesus was allowed to preach in the Jewish Temple. Jesus, on his side, is shown also as acting in a proper manner; he preached in the synagogue when invited, but did not try to attract attention by interrupting ordinary Jewish prayer and rituals. He is described as acting roughly in taking up a whip and turning out money-changers from the Temple outer courtyard but this seems to have commanded at least some degree of support; the Temple police, well-organised and accustomed to keeping order, made no apparent attempt to interfere. Data is lacking for a full description of the incident. He is said to have had a narrow shave at Nazareth when the synagogue congregation, disliking his preaching, attempted to lynch him by throwing him over a cliff; but this was the action of an

hysterical mob, not of educated Pharisees. The only dis-
courteous questions he faced was from a group of Sadducees
who tried to pull his leg about the resurrection of the dead
by asking about a woman who married seven husbands, each
dying in turn: which, in the resurrection, would be her real
husband? This has all the marks of the 'Who was Cain's
wife?' type of question put by the more jocular type of
modern atheist. Jesus gave a stock Pharisaical answer that at
the resurrection people would be like angels and there would
be no marriage. Pharisees who had been listening, it is said,
then came forward with a genuine test question. They asked
what was the greatest commandment of the Torah. Jesus
quoted Deuteronomy: 'You must love the Lord your God
with all your heart, with all your soul, and with all your
mind,'[28] and Leviticus: 'You must love your neighbour as
yourself.'[29] This was a satisfactory answer which showed Jesus
to be, in at least this respect, within the Pharisaical tradition.

While endorsing the Jewish Torah, Jesus did not go out of
his way to follow the more refined interpretations. For
example, the more extreme Pharisees took a ritual wash, up
to the elbows, before eating and ate their meals only in the
company of people of their own kind. Such behaviour was
part of the small change of piety rather as is teetotalism
among the modern kind of Baptist or Methodist. Jesus is
portrayed as repudiating such refinements and arguing that
the way to God should be conceived in more spiritual terms.
His language became positively intemperate: 'Alas for you,
scribes and Pharisees, you hypocrites,' he is quoted as saying.
'You are like whitewashed tombs that look handsome on the
outside, but inside are full of dead men's bones and every
kind of corruption.'[30] The logic of the argument, if not the
manner of its presentation, would have been supported by
many of the orthodox. Jesus is portrayed as putting his
theories into effect by eating with the irreligious and with
prostitutes with no regard for ritual cleanliness. Challenged
by Pharisees, he said his mission was to go after sinners. To

the modern view, this answer appears unimpeachable. There are conservative churchgoers who might murmur against their bishop or evangelical preacher living it up in a strip-tease club but they can have no doctrinal objection to him looking for souls to save in such a place. This would be in line with the general trend of Jesus's thought, even without the specific example he set in the matter. But what if the modern bishop not only ate with prostitutes but also went to bed with them, on the plea of trying to save their souls? He would receive little support and, indeed, in the 1930s an Anglican court condemned the notorious Vicar of Stiffkey who did exactly that and put forward soul-saving as his excuse. To the more pious kind of Jew in Jesus's time, the act of eating was itself a religious rite. It was all right for Jesus to talk to evil-livers to try to convert them but to *eat* with them was, in the eyes of the ultra-pious, an illicit relationship. Naturally Jesus was criticised on this score and he, distrusting the finer interpretations of the Torah and being by nature an outspoken man, retaliated by saying rude things about his critics.

What is certainly clear is that Jesus made few or no converts among the recognised Jewish teachers. Nor, apparently, did he seriously attempt to win them over. The gospels contain no sustained attempt to overthrow six centuries of Jewish tradition and scholarship. Provided the analogy is not pressed too far, Jesus's attitude to official Judaism might be compared with that of the eighteenth century John Wesley to the Church of England. Wesley was a member of that church but rather than attempt, by academic argument, to convert its leaders to his distinctive doctrine, he went out to convert the uneducated masses. Just as Wesley's doctrine of salvation was consistent with the general teaching of the Church of England, but not essential to it, so was Jesus's public teaching consistent with Pharisaical Judaism.

The gospels suggest that Jesus's followers were mostly pious and working class. His leading disciples are represented as fishermen from Lake Tiberias (the 'Sea of Galilee') around the shores of which he did most of his preaching. The regular band was very small; the gospels give figures of twelve and seventy but these should not, possibly, be taken too literally as both have a ritualistic significance. This type of following was not uncharacteristic of an unofficial Galilee rabbi of the period but to point to it as relatively unlettered is not necessarily to impute ignorance on religious matters. Fishing and religion often go together. Many ordinary Galileans of the period were deeply interested in religion, thoroughly conversant with the scriptures and eagerly looking for prophets and for the Christ. They were less hemmed in by the discipline of religious scholarship than were the Jews of Judah, to the south, and so they were good material for such a teacher as Jesus. Undoubtedly Jesus made a strong impression upon this group, as much by his personality as by argument. In addition to the narrow band of personal disciples, Jesus also on occasion addressed what are described as 'multitudes'. These were open air gatherings which, doubtless, assembled more or less casually to hear the new preacher. Jesus told them that the Christ was about to come and that meanwhile they should live virtuous lives: he did not, it seems, make any attempt to organise them or to enroll them into any definite sect.

He must have been a transient figure, a passing curiosity. According to the chronology of the gospels, Jesus taught at most for three years and possibly for as little as one year. What would have happened if he had gone on for the span of his normal lifetime, is unknowable.

But he had hardly got started before he was executed.

[1] Mk 1:15	[11] Is 61:1-2	[21] Mt 5:22
[2] Lk 17:21	[12] Mt 5:6	[22] Mt 5:28
[3] Mt 24:34	[13] Prov 21:21	[23] Mt 5:34
[4] Mt 16:18	[14] Ps 42:1	[24] Mt 5:39
[5] Ex 20:17	[15] Mt 5:7	[25] Mt 5:43-44
[6] Mt 5:3	[16] Mt 5:8	[26] Mt 5:29-30
[7] Mt 5:5	[17] Ps 24:3-4	[27] Mt 23:1-4
[8] Ps 37:11	[18] Mt 5:9	[28] Deut 6:5
[9] Mt 5:4	[19] Mt 5:10	[29] Lev 19:18
[10] Ps 126:5	[20] Mt 5:17-18	[30] Mt 23:27

V

The Execution of Jesus

AT some date between the years A.D. 26 and 36, Jesus of Nazareth was executed by being hung up on a cross at Jerusalem. (The dates are those when Pontius Pilate was Prefect of Judaea.) It was a painful, ignominious form of death which, it is unanimously reported, Jesus accepted with dignity. By any measure, this was one of the leading events in the recent history of the human race. The world's biggest religion, Christianity, could not have come into existence without it; had Jesus died a natural death, its theology would be radically different even if it had started at all.

Unfortunately the evidence about this event is gravely defective and it is impossible to construct a watertight historical account of it. The scholars are in disagreement about it. Some people have gone so far as to claim that it is entirely fabulous but, for the present purposes, it is assumed that it did really take place. Its reality is endorsed by the fact that it is not the kind of story that any Jewish sect would make up about its hero. To the first Christians the crucifixion was an embarrassment which had to be explained away. The Book of Deuteronomy states 'One who has been hanged is accursed of God.'[1] It was not until the seventh century that the cross became the normal Christian symbol.

As a preliminary to considering it, the first point must be to ascertain what legal offence, if any, Jesus committed. One view, often expressed popularly, is that he claimed to be God Almighty and this so offended the Jewish authorities that they got the Roman occupying power to execute him.

Had Jesus in fact claimed to be God, the Jewish authorities might well have reacted in some such way and not only the authorities but all pious Jews of every kind, Pharisees, Essenes, sectarians. The cardinal feature of the Jewish religion was belief in the single, invisible Yahweh. This belief was protected by elaborate rules about blasphemy, rules designed to prevent any kind of insult to Yahweh or any attempt to put him on a level with the gods of other religions. (It must be remembered that Judaism was constantly fighting to defend its own purity against powerful rival cults.) By Jesus's time it counted as blasphemy even to speak the name of Yahweh. The penalty for grave blasphemy, plainly laid down in Jewish law, was to be stoned to death; this form of execution avoided the executioners having personal contact with so unpleasant a person. For a man to claim to be God would be the worst blasphemy that could be imagined and there could be no doubt about the penalty. Nor, as in a twentieth century court, could there be any excuse of mental derangement; madness was equated with possession by evil spirits who might well, in such a serious case, be dealt with by stoning the man they had entered.

In fact Jesus did not publicly claim to be God and there is no explicit statement either in the gospels or in the later parts of the New Testament that he was God. Paul of Tarsus did not teach, in unambiguous terms, that Jesus was God and the sect of Jewish Christians, which persisted for three or four centuries, did not claim divinity for Jesus. There are a good many phrases in the New Testament which are consistent with the divinity of Jesus, particularly in John's gospel, but this is not the same as saying that they positively state it. Such phrases, in any event, have nothing to do with what Jesus said to the general public. If he did hint that he was divine, he did so only in private to his immediate followers. The weight of probability must be that he made no such claim at all and that the doctrine of Jesus as God was devised by men looking back on him after his execution.

What, then, did Jesus claim to be?

In the early part of his teaching career he implied that he was a man with a special mission from Yahweh to preach the coming of the 'Kingdom'. He claimed to speak with direct authority and not just on the basis of scholarship and interpretation. Within the Jewish religion, such a claim is readily comprehensible. The prophets of the Old Testament had claimed such authority and so did a few teachers in Jesus's time, for example John the Baptist. It was a recognised phenomenon, disliked by some and eagerly welcomed by others.

Then, at a late stage, according to the gospels, he claimed to be the Christ—the miraculous ruler sent from God to inaugurate the new 'Kingdom'. He was not only herald of the Kingdom but its ruler. He did not use this claim in his ordinary public teaching. It is reported that when Peter privately called him the Christ, he specifically enjoined silence on the subject. Jesus's only public claim to be the Christ was made when he was already on trial before the Jewish Sanhedrin.

Now Jesus at this stage plainly was not the Christ in any sense that fitted Jewish prophecies. He was not the Christ any more than Martin Luther was Pope of Rome. The Christ was to be a powerful and just ruler, equipped with a plenitude of divine strength; or, alternatively, some saw him as a miraculous military leader who would lead the Jews to victory. He was not to be just a preacher and healer as Jesus was.

Why, then, did Jesus make a claim which was so patently absurd?

There are three possible explanations.

The first is that his mind was unhinged by religious mania. This is possible and there have been many such cases. But it is an inherently unattractive theory and the weight of probability must be against it if only for the reason that the remainder of his teachings and behaviour do not reflect insanity. Allowing for the context in which he lived, his words and actions were rational and showed a quick, acute intelligence.

Secondly, it can be hazarded that he made no claim at all to be the Christ. This would be in keeping with the greater part of his teachings. He was executed for some reason which is now unknown, perhaps in some brush with the Romans who were ready to resort to capital punishment with very little pretext. After his death his followers decided he was the Christ and put words into his mouth; they expected him to come back from the dead at any moment to rule as the Christ of Jewish prophesy. This theory short-cuts most of the difficulties of the gospel accounts and may well be the best that can be adduced.

There is, however, a third theory which must carry weight because it is the one upon which the whole Christian tradition from the beginning has been based. Moreover it makes use of the gospel accounts, which appear inherently unlikely to have been entirely a fabrication. It is that having preached his doctrines in Galilee, Jesus went up to Jerusalem with the specific intention of claiming to be the Christ and of risking being executed. One version of this theory is that he was deliberately provoking his own execution. The point of this procedure was to enable him to return from the dead as the Christ endued with the plenitude of divine power. Or, conceivably, he might have expected a divine intervention during his execution which would turn him into the proper Christ without him actually dying. Whatever the inner psychology and motivation of Jesus—evidence about it is wholly lacking—there can be no doubt on the central point that if a man went around claiming to be the Christ, the miraculous leader of the Jews, the Romans would be liable to arrest him and crucify him. It must be remembered that Palestine was boiling up towards the great Jewish revolts.

According to this theory, Jesus was preaching in the Temple and arousing the interest of his audiences. The gospel

accounts actually have him making a ceremonial entry into
Jerusalem on a donkey, as had been prophesied for the
Messiah. While making no outright claim, he was hinting
that the Christ was about to come and that terrible things
were about to happen. His words, as quoted, take on the
characteristic tinge of the eschatological Judaism of the time
as in the Book of Daniel and the scrolls of the Qumran sect.
'. . . And then the sign of the Son of Man shall appear in
heaven; then too all the peoples of the earth will beat their
breasts; and they will see the Son of Man coming on the
clouds of heaven with power and great glory. And he will
send his angels with a loud trumpet to gather his chosen from
the four winds . . .'[2] Whether or not Jesus actually spoke such
words does not matter too much—they were a routine piece
of eschatology which could well have been put into his mouth
by an editor. The point is that by the unanimous account of
the gospels he was speaking in this general vein. Such words,
inevitably, excited the people, worried the Temple authorities and, above all, angered the Romans who wanted no talk
of angels and trumpets to interfere with their power. Jesus
also spoke of the destruction of Jerusalem and of the Temple,
a point which must have worried the Jewish authorities more
than it did the Romans. This in fact did happen about thirty-
five years later and some scholars have argued that the fore-
casts were put into the gospels after the event so as to add to
Jesus's reputation. But such forgery is not the necessary
explanation. Jesus lived in an atmosphere of political religious
ferment and a man of his sensitivity might well have had a
flash of mixed judgment and prevision in which he saw
Jerusalem destroyed. Were a modern preacher to declare in
prophetic utterance that within twenty-five years not one
stone of New York would stand upon another, he would be
backing a reasonable outside chance.

During the greater part of his teaching, which had been in
Galilee, Jesus had had no contact with Roman authority.
Galilee was a semi-independent country under its own ruler,

Herod Antipas, a son of Herod the Great. When Jesus is depicted healing the daughter of a worthy centurion, it must have been a centurion in Herod's army, not in the main Roman army. Herod was definitely a puppet of the Romans and he was much disliked by the more nationalist of his subjects; he was alleged to be impious and immoral and the story is that he executed John the Baptist as a kind of after-dinner prank. Although he was a member of the Jewish faith, men such as Jesus and his followers would see no room for him in the Kingdom of Heaven. Nevertheless there is no evidence that Jesus followed John the Baptist in specifically preaching against Herod or stirring up the people against him. So far as Herod was concerned, Jesus was just another religious visionary and he probably had never even heard of him. At this stage, it must be remembered, Jesus was not claiming to be the Christ.

Judaea, on the other hand, was a Roman province ruled by a Roman Prefect appointed by the Emperor. By unanimous tradition, this Prefect was Pontius Pilate and as the next stage in considering the circumstances of Jesus's execution it is necessary to examine Pilate and the administration he represented. That Pilate really existed has been conclusively proved by archaeologists digging up in the ruins of his capital, Caesarea, a stone inscribed 'Pontius Pilatus Praefectus Judaea'.

What kind of man was Pilate?

Roman administration in this period was so regular that it is possible to adduce a good deal about him. Prefects were invariably chosen from among regimental commanders in the army. In a few cases they might have risen from the ranks but normally they belonged to the Roman minor gentry. There is an old legend to the effect that Pilate was the son of a German princeling who had entered the Roman service but this is improbable: non-Romans did not at this early date serve as army officers. His name does not suggest that he was a naturalised citizen and fits best a native of central Italy.

Such a man as Pilate did not belong to the higher Roman aristocracy, to the senatorial families, and he was very much an official holding power by favour of the Emperor in what was a very new system of government.

He must have been an able or even a brilliant man. The gospels indicate that he was a 'Friend of Caesar'; this was an honorific title bestowed by the Emperor upon people who had served him well and in case of misconduct it could be withdrawn. Had Pilate received a letter from Rome which omitted the formula 'Friend of Caesar' he would realise that he had fallen into ill favour. Judaea, headquarters of the powerful and turbulent Jewish religion, was possibly the most difficult province in the Roman Empire and for this reason alone it can be surmised that Pilate was an able man. He belonged to the class which had made and sustained the Roman Empire and had made his way more by merit than by birth.

In the Roman administration, military and civil functions were closely intertwined. The power of the Emperor depended largely on the fact that he was commander-in-chief of the army and, indeed, the Latin title of Imperator was originally a military rank. Commissioned officers, who were relatively few in numbers (only twenty or so for a legion of 6,000 men), were administrators who could move readily between civil and military duties. The quick path to fame was to win battles but civil governorships offered dignity and some degree of financial reward, although there were laws against extorting too much money from a subject population.

Over all in his province, save those who held Roman citizenship, Pilate's powers were absolute. He could, if he wished, order an execution at his whim and without formality. The only check on him was that his subjects might send a mission to Rome to complain of him to the Emperor, and this in Pilate's case the Jewish authorities did and he was dismissed. (Also Pilate was subordinate to the Emperor's personal representative in the region, the Legate at Antioch.)

A Roman Prefect was not a Governor in the sense that he conducted any detailed administration of his province. He had no elaborate bureaucracy under him and few executive assistants. He had no police force. If people disobeyed him he used his army; two legions were stationed in Judaea, many of the rank and file doubtless locally recruited although no strict Jew would serve. A Roman Prefect maintained basic law and order, saw to the collection of taxes for Rome (the detailed work of assessment and collection was farmed out to local contractors) and perhaps tried to inaugurate some public construction by which he would be remembered—a road, a bridge, a water supply system. Roman Prefects appear to have had a particular penchant for the introduction of running water. For the rest, the Prefect was available to hear complaints from people and to settle disputes; he sat frequently on his 'tribunal' in public in the open air to hear whatever was brought before him. Such sessions started at dawn.

In Judaea, as in other imperial provinces, the local civic authorities continued to function and were more influential in the life of the ordinary person than was the Roman Prefect. The system might be compared with the twentieth century British colonial system of 'indirect rule' through tribal chiefs in Africa. The point at which the Romans interfered with the local authorities was that the power of executing a death sentence was normally reserved to themselves. When a local authority wanted to execute a criminal, they had to take him before the Prefect. This was an obvious safeguard without which the local authorities would have been able to get rid of pro-Romans at will. It existed across the empire as the ordinary rule of administration but there is at least some doubt about whether it was fully applied in Judaea. Jewish law laid down a range of offences which were punishable by death together with the procedures for hearing them and the various modes of execution, which were strangulation, hanging by the neck and stoning. There is no clear indication in Jewish documents that at the time of Jesus the Jewish authorities had ceased to exercise such jurisdiction. Certainly fragments still survive of a notice which threatened death to any non-Jew who entered the inner part of the Temple and this would seem to indicate at least some capital jurisdiction by the Jewish authorities. Perhaps the best guess is that in the case of the elaborate and powerful Jewish religion the Romans gave the Jews a general dispensation to execute people for certain classes of religious offence. The martyr Stephen is described in the Acts of the Apostles of having been executed by stoning without any reference to the Roman authorities. Political offences, however, must have remained within the sole power of the Prefect.

Pilate was a harsh, energetic man who believed that the Jewish religion should be subordinated to Roman imperial power. The Romans, it must be recalled, were themselves very religious and took it that the gods and rites of Rome had caused their great success in the world. The Roman gods had conquered other gods. Local deities and rites in different parts of the empire were automatically tolerated but to a strict Roman they were second-rate affairs and various attempts were made to fit them into a subordinate place in the Roman religious system. A Roman could safely honour such gods without derogation of his own deities. The idea was also propagated that the chief Roman god, Jupiter (the same as the Greek Zeus), was the ultimate father of the world and superior to all other deities. Obviously the Jewish Yahweh could not be fitted into such a system. If it was put to a pious Jew that Yahweh had failed against the gods of Rome, the answer came back that failure was not to be measured in solely political terms and that, anyway, Yahweh was soon going to defeat everyone else by sending the Christ and ending the existing world order. Yahweh was not conquered but merely biding his time. Moreover, the Jews, especially the Pharisees, were insisting that Yahweh was the

only God and that no other deities existed at all; the only
other invisible beings were various angels and spirits that
Yahweh had created. Such a line of argument obviously
annoyed the Romans and, although they tolerated Jews and
allowed them exemptions from public duties involving contact with idolatry, Judaism could not fit easily into the Roman
system. Pilate, although he is said to have married a Jewish
wife, took little account of the complexities of the Jewish
religion and believed in hitting it hard when it looked
dangerous.

He had an early brush with the Jews when he marched a
legion into Jerusalem so that its standards, with idols on
them, were in sight of the Temple. The Jews regarded this as
an appalling insult to Yahweh. They sent a deputation to
protest to Pilate at Caesarea. When Pilate temporised they
flung themselves on the floor and said they would rather be
killed than leave his presence without getting their way.
Pilate gave in and thereafter when Roman legions entered
Jerusalem they left their standards behind. (The episode
appears to have been a deliberate challenge by Pilate to the
Jews, not just an accident.)

Later Pilate, in characteristic Roman vein, decided to
improve Jerusalem's water supply by building an aqueduct.
To pay for it he took treasure from the Temple. Now the
Temple was a wealthy institution, financed by an annual tax
from Jews throughout the empire; the Romans endorsed the
collection of this tax. The proceeds were supposed to be used
partly for religious purposes and partly for such things as
aqueducts. Pilate, as civil ruler, might well have reckoned
that he was entitled to use some of the money for civil purposes but most Jews regarded his action as theft. There were
protest demonstrations and attacks on Pilate's workmen,
doubtless with Zealots from Galilee playing a part. Pilate
retaliated by getting his soldiers to dress in plain clothes, mix
in with the demonstrators and then pull out swords and start
to kill, terrorise and disperse them. It was an ingenious

method of putting down a demonstration but it seems to have got out of hand. Over 1,000 Jews were killed and Pilate became correspondingly the more unpopular.

The Jewish aristocracy of the Sadducee party was in an ambivalent position. Many of them tolerated Roman suzerainty as the least available evil. Within the Roman system the Jews did, after all, have the benefit of belonging to an extensive civilisation and they were free to practise their religion. Regular sacrifices were offered in the Temple on the Emperor's behalf. Many Pharisees, too, while abominating pagan Rome were content to await the Day of the Lord and meanwhile refrain from physical resistance. In the context of the moment, Pilate and the Jewish authorities were in a state of balance, each depending upon moderation in the other. Pilate appointed the High Priest but could choose only from a narrow group of families. The Jews had control over their own religious affairs but only for as long as they did not resist Rome. The balance was continually in danger of being upset by waves of popular agitation and unofficial violence and such a Galilean prophet as Jesus was the kind of person who was automatically labelled a troublemaker. The fear of revolution was a legitimate one, not imaginary. There were continual episodes of disorder and the Zealot party made a habit of assassinating Jews whom they regarded as Quislings; within thirty-five years, it must be repeated, the Jews were to stage the only nationalistic revolt which ever took place within the Roman Empire.

The High Priest was the titular head of the Jewish religion and he exerted high power and patronage. He was as much a political as a religious figure and within living memory the holder of his office had been the actual ruler of the country. The High Priest was chairman of the Sanhedrin which was partly a legislative body and partly a court of law; it worked according to strict rules of procedure and was divided into various parties and factions. By Jesus's time the Pharisees appear to have been greatly increasing their influence in it

7

but the majority were still Sadducees. Membership of the Sanhedrin appears to have been for life and recruitment was partly by co-option and partly by popular election. While it was not in the modern sense a 'democratic' body, it can be counted as broadly representative of the leading trends of Jewish thought. Members of the Sanhedrin were men of status and of learning.

According to the gospels, Jesus, after teaching for a short time in Jerusalem, was arrested and brought before the High Priest and the Sanhedrin. The session took place at night. Jesus claimed to be the Christ and the Sanhedrin condemned him to death for blasphemy and sent him on to Pilate for the sentence to be confirmed. When the death sentence was passed, members of the Sanhedrin insulted him and spat at him.

This is a strange story which does not tie up with other known facts.

If it was nothing else, the Sanhedrin was a formal, even pedantic body which acted according to strict rules of procedure. The idea of it meeting in a hurry in the middle of the night to settle a capital charge with profound religious implications is palpably improbable. It was no more in the habit of acting in that way than is the United States Supreme Court. The additional ornament, that the judges spat at a man they had just condemned to death, is even more bizarre.

The traditional Christian explanation has been that the Sanhedrin was acting in a hurry because it wanted to get Jesus executed before the Passover Feast which was due to start the next evening. But why the hurry? Jesus could perfectly well have been remanded in the Temple prison until the feast was over. If it is claimed that the High Priest was fearful of his popularity among the people, then to take him out and publicly execute him was as likely to arouse trouble as to hold him in gaol. In any case, the members of the Sanhedrin were grave men, occupied with the injunctions of the Torah; they would have been concerned with ritual preparations for the great feast rather than with any criminal trial. Would a modern Roman Catholic court be disposed to hear a case on Christmas Day? In the case of the Sanhedrin members, there was actual danger of ritual pollution which would have been a serious nuisance on the eve of the feast.

Anyway, was Jesus convicted by the Sanhedrin of any offence which carried the death penalty by Jewish law?

The answer is in the negative. Jesus claimed to be the Christ. While this was doubtless profoundly irritating to Jewish judges who did not believe him, it was not a grave blasphemy punishable by death: Jewish law was pedantic about such matters. At most it came within the category of minor blasphemy which, according to the Torah, should be dealt with either by a flogging or by being left for the judgment of God. According to the gospels, Jesus couched his claim in wholly scriptural terms, quoting the Book of Daniel.

To claim to be the Christ was not something that could get Jesus legally executed by Jews. But it was, of course, a claim that could readily expose Jesus to arbitrary execution by Pontius Pilate.

So what was the point of the Sanhedrin procedure if it took place on roughly the lines portrayed in the gospels?

It becomes much more comprehensible if it is regarded not as a trial but as an inquiry. If it is supposed that Jesus had been arrested on Roman authority and was to be tried by Pilate at the normal 'tribunal' session at dawn the next morning, it is easy to understand the Sanhedrin meeting hurriedly in the night to inquire into the case. Jesus was, after all, a Jewish teacher who had been prominent in the Temple and had acquired at least some following. Nothing would be more natural than for the Jewish authorities to be interested in his case and in getting at the facts before Pilate did. One difficulty with this supposition is that the first three gospels, the synoptics, tell of Jesus being arrested by Jewish police, not by Roman soldiers. However, John's gospel, which reflects a different strain of tradition, says that Jesus was arrested by a 'cohort' which is the technical term for a squad of the regular Roman army. If John's account is correct, the Roman authorities must have been involved in the arrest.

At this point the theory that the Sanhedrin hearing was an inquiry and not a trial diverges into two different possibilities, between which there is little to choose.

One theory is that the Sanhedrin was anxious to save Jesus from execution by the Romans but that he spoiled any chance of it being able to do this by stating in terms that he was the Christ, an offence for which Pilate would execute him. The High Priest tore his clothes as a sign of mourning at Jesus's obstinate attitude and impending death. (Had Jesus committed grave blasphemy, punishable by death under Jewish law, the whole assembly and not just the High Priest would have torn their clothes.)

The alternative theory is that the Jewish authorities were willing, from time to time, to placate the Romans by handing them a religious criminal of small importance. Properly managed, such a policy would please the Romans without doing any harm to Judaism. This ties in with the gospel portrayal of the Sanhedrin leaders subsequently prosecuting Jesus before Pilate. The preliminary inquiry in the night was to establish whether Jesus was a suitable person to be handed over in this way and to get the facts about him. Of course the formal responsibility would remain Roman; the situation would be Jewish leaders accusing a fellow Jew of a Roman offence before a Roman judge. This kind of thing seems to have happened from time to time and is, indeed, an almost inevitable feature of occupation of a country by a foreign power.

After the Sanhedrin hearing, whatever its exact nature, Jesus apparently was taken for trial before Pontius Pilate.

Strictly, Pilate was bound by no procedural obligations. In dealing with such a non-Roman as Jesus he could conduct the trial however he chose or even order an execution with no hearing at all. However Roman Prefects customarily followed the spirit of Roman legal forms even when they were not bound to do so and, according to the gospels, Pilate seems to have done so in the case of Jesus. He sat in the open air in public with a crowd looking on and able to barrack and shout advice. This was normal. Under Roman law if a prisoner pleaded guilty, the judge had to repeat the charge to him before passing sentence and this, according to the gospels, Pilate did to Jesus. The sentence itself, to be scourged and crucified, followed the normal Roman form; many hundreds of Jews were at one time and another crucified by the Romans for political reasons.

The point of course is that Jesus made no attempt to defend himself. By claiming to be the Christ, the King of the Jews, he was automatically committing treason against Rome. Pilate, who cannot have been a fool, obviously thought he was dealing with an unusual type of case. Jesus was claiming to be a king but there were around him none of the trappings of armed rebellion or political power. He was just another Jewish preacher. Yet Pilate seems to have treated him seriously and not to have dismissed him as weak in the head. When Jesus, according to John, said: 'Mine is not a kingdom of this world',[3] Pilate was impressed, although mystified. It was easy to suppose that Jesus, with his firm conviction that he was the Christ and was soon to receive a plenitude of divine power, was an impressive prisoner. Pilate tried to find a way out by ordering Jesus to be whipped and released. This was a normal Roman provincial procedure in cases which were not fully proven and which the judge did not take too seriously; the whipping—a relatively light one with rods, not the savage scourging with clubs—was administered as a warning. According to the gospels, the bystanders objected to such lenient treatment and Pilate thereupon took the formally correct course of ordering Jesus to be scourged and executed. It was one of probably dozens of death sentences Pilate had passed and he was unlikely to have been the kind of man who worried about it. The gospels have him washing his hands, in a symbolic gesture, and telling the bystanders that the responsibility was theirs.

There is nothing inherently impossible about such a scene but it must be remembered that the gospel narratives were written at a time when Christianity was separating from Judaism and was in conflict with it. It would be natural for the writers to stress the Jewish role in the crucifixion and to minimise the Roman responsibility. So the bystanders, represented as Jews antagonistic to Jesus, are given a decisive role and made to say the improbable words: 'His blood be on us and on our children.'[4] There is also the curious episode of Barabbas. According to the gospels, it was customary for the Romans to release a Jewish prisoner at the time of the Passover festival. Pilate offered to release Jesus but the bystanders insisted that the pardon should go to Barabbas. Apart from the fact that there is no independent evidence from either Roman or Jewish sources that such a custom even existed, the story smells more of ritual than of real history. Barabbas in Hebrew means 'son of a father' and his first name is given in some early gospel manuscripts as 'Jesus'. It is possible to guess at several different meanings for the Barabbas story but for the present purpose it is sufficient to observe that there may well be more to it than meets the eye.

The death sentence, as was customary, was carried out immediately.

First Jesus was scourged. This was the normal preliminary to crucifixion and was a brutal affair carried out with clubs. The scourging alone was enough to break a man. Then he was taken to the public execution place and hung up to die. The gospel accounts say that two thieves were executed at the same time.

Although many thousands of crucifixions were carried out in the ancient world, there is no contemporary account of exactly how they were done and no contemporary picture. The earliest Christian representations date from about two centuries after the punishment had been abolished. It is a safe assumption, however, that if only for anatomical reasons the traditional Christian artistic convention is incorrect; this has been discovered by sculptors who, in making life-sized models, have found it difficult to make the figure stay on the cross. The real procedure probably varied at different times and places but it is credible to suppose that an upright post was permanently in position at a regular place of execution and that the victim was fixed to a crossbar and then lifted up on to the post. The result is more likely to have been a T rather than a + shape. If nails were used, it would have been no use putting them through the victim's palms because the flesh there is not strong enough to support the weight of the body; they would have had to have been knocked through the victim's wrists. Roman iron nails, of which plenty of specimens still exist, were large, jagged things and to drive them into a man was in itself an act of extreme brutality. Often a victim was tied to the crossbar, not nailed, and this would appear to be an easier and more reliable way of supporting him. Or perhaps both nails and rope were used. The most effective way of fixing a man to a crossbar is to stretch his arms backwards over it so that it runs under his armpits; as a simple test can show, this is an acutely painful position but a secure one. There would have been no need to fix the feet to the upright post but it seems that a peg was sometimes driven between the victim's legs to give some extra support. Of course the representation of Jesus as nailed to the cross by his hands and feet does not come from the gospels but from later Christian reflection upon such texts as 'They will look on one whom they have pierced'[5] in the Book of Zechariah.

To be hung up upon a cross and just left to die in public is the most contemptuous form of execution that can be imagined. It was reserved for slaves and people of low class. Eventually Christianity was to find a symbolic value in it—

the suffering saviour stretched out in the view of every passer-by—but at the time it was a humiliating disgrace and early Christians actually got laughed at because their founder had been crucified. The earliest known picture of the crucifixion is a satirical drawing which shows the victim with a donkey's head. (It was found in the Roman catacombs and was designed, presumably, as anti-Christian propaganda.) Also it was a painful, lingering death and sometimes the victim lasted as long as three days. The drawing of every breath was agonising and the eventual cause of death was probably sheer exhaustion, either heart failure or asphyxiation from the victim being too tired to breathe. There was a guild of religious women in Jerusalem in Jesus's time which comforted condemned criminals by giving them a pain-reducing drug and this, according to the gospels, seems to have been offered to Jesus.

Because of the difficulty of breathing, the victim could not have spoken distinctly on the cross and the last words of Jesus, as recorded in the gospels, must be allowed ritual rather than historical significance. (Anyway the accounts vary.) The words 'My God, my God, why have you deserted me?'[6] have been taken by some to mean that at the last moment Jesus despaired of his mission when he realised that there was going to be no miraculous intervention to save him. Actually they are the opening words of Psalm 22, which is often recited in the presence of death. Devout Jews spoke it in Adolf Hitler's extermination camps in the present century. It is credible, and indeed probable, that such a devout Jew as Jesus would, in his last agony, find comfort in repeating to himself the awesome words of this psalm, which go on from despair to triumph.

'My God, my God, why have you deserted me?
How far from saving me, the words I groan!
I call all day, my God, but you never answer,
all night long I call and cannot rest.

Yet, Holy One, you
who make your home in the praises of Israel,
in you our fathers put their trust,
they trusted and you rescued them;
they called to you for help and they were saved,
they never trusted you in vain.
Yet here am I, now more worm than man,
scorn of mankind, jest of the people,
all who see me jeer at me,
they toss their heads and sneer,
"He relied on Yahweh, let Yahweh save him!
If Yahweh is his friend, let Him rescue him . . ."
. . . I am like water draining away,
my bones are all disjointed,
my heart is like wax,
melting inside me;
my palate is drier than a potsherd
and my tongue is stuck to my jaw.
A pack of dogs surrounds me,
a gang of villains closes me in;
they tie me hand and foot
and leave me lying in the dust of death.
I can count every one of my bones,
and there they glare at me, gloating;
they divide my garments among them
and cast lots for my clothes.
Do not stand aside, Yahweh.
O my strength, come quickly to my help;
rescue my soul from the sword,
my dear life from the paw of the dog . . .
. . . The whole earth, from end to end, will remember and
    come back to Yahweh;
all the families of the nations will bow down before him.
For Yahweh reigns, the ruler of nations!
Before him all the prosperous of the earth will bow down,
before him will bow all who go down to the dust.

And my soul will live for him, my children will serve him;
men will proclaim the Lord for generations still to come,
his righteousness to a people yet unborn. All this he has
done.'

This was the frame of mind in which Jesus of Nazareth met
his death and these words may well have been his last conscious thoughts.

[1] Deut 21:23   [3] Jn 18:36   [5] Zech 12:10
[2] Mt 24:30–31   [4] Mt 27:25   [6] Mt 27:46

VI

The Original Sect

THE history of Christianity began, so far as can be ascertained, with a Jewish sect in Jerusalem which looked forward to the imminent coming of the Christ, a miraculous personality who would overturn the existing world order. The members believed that the Christ had already made a preliminary appearance in the person of Jesus of Nazareth and was soon to come again properly. They looked back upon Jesus as their unique prophet and teacher and Jesus's brother, James the Just, was among their leaders. They were a devout group with members of both sexes who prayed frequently and, perhaps, held their property in common. Some of the members were prone to dreams and visions and some were inspired to act as prophets. There were stories of miraculous cures taking place through the group's intercession. Undoubtedly they were an agitated, intense community and they believed they possessed a special revelation from God. It is difficult to be certain about dates but it can be reckoned that the group was soundly established before the fall of Jerusalem in A.D. 70 and had then existed for over thirty years.

Exactly what the group called itself is not clear. The name 'Christian' was not in use at all in the first days—it was devised not in Jerusalem but in Syrian Antioch. There is some reason to suppose that in view of their attitude to possessions they were sometimes termed, simply, 'The Poor', but since this was also applied to the Essenes it can lead to confusion. The most straightforward term for them at this very first stage is 'Disciples of Jesus', it being normal for a Jewish group to be named in this way after the teacher who had founded it.

Obviously the Disciples of Jesus were akin to other Jewish sects, particularly to the Essenes of Qumran. Like the Essenes they looked back to a 'Teacher of Righteousness' and forward to the coming of the Christ. Both groups claimed to possess a special revelation from God. Both groups attached importance to renouncing personal possessions. Their special rituals had much in common, both groups eating ceremonial meals and initiating recruits with a ceremonial washing. Since the Essenes were by far the older group it is reasonable to suppose that the resemblances were not a coincidence but resulted from the newer group deliberately taking over some of the older one's practices. But the Essenes and the Disciples of Jesus were far from identical. They differed even on such a central matter as the Jewish Temple. The Disciples of Jesus continued to worship at the Temple and to sacrifice there, whereas the Essenes totally repudiated it. The Essenes expected two Christs to appear, neither of them identical with the Teacher of Righteousness; the Disciples of Jesus expected only one Christ and identified him with Jesus. The Essenes were a largely male brotherhood with no proper place for women; the Disciples of Jesus included many women and one of the key factors in the future spread of Christianity was to be its appeal to the female sex.

There were resemblances, too, between the Disciples of Jesus and the militant sect of the Zealots, who were to be prominent in the Jewish revolts. The Zealots looked forward confidently to the appearance of the Christ and, indeed, based their military strategy upon the assumption that he was going to appear. However they were less patient than the Disciples of Jesus and were willing to hurry things along by striking against the orthodox Jewish leadership and the occupying Roman power: the Disciples of Jesus took up a more passive attitude, although some of them may well have fought with the Zealots and taken part in the final defence of Masada.

It is a reasonably safe assumption that the three groups— Essenes, Zealots and Disciples of Jesus—had so much in common that many members drifted from one to another. The Disciples of Jesus was the smallest and the newest of the three. In all probability there were also other sects, based upon particular teachers, which put forward different views about the Christ but were a part of the general ferment.

The Disciples of Jesus looked back upon their founder, thought about him and, in process of time, developed an elaborate theology about him, the process hastened by visions and prophetic utterance. It was a dynamic, evolving sect. Unfortunately the members were not interested in historical information about Jesus in the modern sense but in setting him into a cosmic perspective. The miraculous side of him was all-important and the human side hardly counted at all. It is because all information about Jesus derives from this visionary sect that it is so difficult to deal with him historically. With a fair degree of certainty it can be stated what the Disciples of Jesus believed and taught but because of their nature this cannot be the same thing as scientific history.

For example, the Disciples of Jesus believed that Jesus had been seen alive again after his crucifixion but it is impossible to get to the bottom of the story. The accounts in the gospels are different and inconsistent.

It is useless to approach the resurrection in search of an entirely 'rational' explanation. Some have tried to argue that Jesus was taken down from the cross while he was still alive and that he afterwards recovered. It has been suggested that the draught he was given to drink was a narcotic which helped along such a process. Alternatively, it has been suggested that his followers removed his body from the tomb and then pretended he had risen from the dead. The weakness of such explanations is that they are unsupported by positive evidence, are inherently improbable and do not fit the psychological mood of the Disciples of Jesus. The only safe assumption is that if Jesus was crucified he was crucified properly and died of it.

A more satisfactory approach is to look at the doctrine of the resurrection of the dead, which was a central part of Pharisaical Judaism. All the prophets of the Christ, including Jesus and his followers, believed in it. They saw death as a temporary state. Obviously anyone who passionately believes in such a doctrine is liable to become excited, or even hysterical about it. The idea of dead men leaving their graves was part of the context of the coming of the Christ. Jesus was specifically credited with raising a man called Lazarus from the dead; the implication is that Lazarus, after being resurrected went on to live an ordinary human life and this was much more striking than the form of resurrection attributed to Jesus himself. The Essenes very probably believed in communication with the dead. The gospel of Matthew claims that at the moment of Jesus's death on the cross 'the tombs opened and the bodies of many holy men rose from the dead'.[1]

People who believe in ghosts and think about ghosts often see ghosts. Undoubtedly there are certain paranormal powers of the mind which have been described throughout human history and have not yet been properly defined. Given a context of excitement over resurrection of the dead, people are liable to see and hear unusual things. This, surely, can be taken as axiomatic. Moreover Jesus himself appears to have been an individual of exceptionally powerful personality who exerted a strong impact.

Jesus's followers believed that they saw Jesus alive again. He did not come back as an ordinary human being but had a special kind of body which could materialise and dematerialise. The process was a discreet one and did not involve dramatic public appearances such as would have thrown the general public into consternation. For example, there was no belief that Jesus went back to preaching in the

Temple—had he done so, and been proved to be the man who had been crucified, the implications would indeed be shattering. The earliest extant account of the experiences, that in Paul's first letter to the Corinthians, contains no account of an empty tomb but says that the dead Jesus has appeared to various people including Paul himself. (Paul draws no distinction between his own encounter with the risen Jesus and the appearances immediately after the crucifixion.) The gospel accounts bring in the empty tomb but are inconsistent on the details of it; the line of argument may well have been that Jesus had appeared, therefore there must be an empty tomb, therefore, in order to convince doubters, an empty tomb must be described. In other words, the empty tomb was the result and not the cause of the resurrection story. Of course this leaves unanswered the question of what *did* happen to Jesus's body. Conceivably it could have been thrown into a common pit for executed criminals but information is lacking.

All that can be stated for certain about the resurrection is that a small group of people really believed it had happened and that the right psychological conditions existed for such a belief. It made no immediate impact on Judaism outside this narrow group. The New Testament accounts are so inconsistent and cursory that it is impossible to construct a watertight narrative out of them. The appearances continued sporadically for some time but had only an indirect influence upon the development of the Christian church; the risen Jesus did not preach but he inspired Paul of Tarsus to preach.

With the passing of time, the resurrection became more and more central to Christian theology and was held, indeed, to be the central fact in the dealings of God with man. For practical purposes it became more important than the doctrine of the coming of the Christ and, indeed, it came to be held that the Christ had come already. The second coming of Jesus would be a finishing-off process, not the beginning. It took about a century for this type of thought to evolve and by the time it was complete Christianity was a recognisably separate religion from Judaism.

Some would say that the process depended entirely upon the thought and inspiration of Jesus's followers. On the other hand, Christians of the more orthodox kind would claim that the process was already implicit in Jesus's own teachings and that Jesus had explicitly laid down the more important points. For example, the gospels attribute to Jesus definite words that his blood would be shed to redeem men's sins. For the present purpose it does not matter too much to try to distinguish in detail between what Jesus taught and what his followers were teaching a century later. Obviously it is wrong to suppose that Jesus put forward cut and dried Christianity and then commissioned his followers to spread it; such a theory breaks down on the elementary point that the main teacher of Christianity, Paul of Tarsus, never met Jesus except in visions. Equally obviously, the early disciples appear to have revered Jesus and so would not consciously have sought to teach in opposition to him. What matters for present purposes is that a particular complex of doctrine, that of Christianity, arose from an interaction between Jesus's own teachings and the thoughts of his first followers after his death.

The source for almost all Christian doctrine, save that Jesus was God, was Jewish. ('Jewish' includes of course sectarian Judaism of the time and not just what became Jewish orthodoxy in the future.) For example, the Disciples of Jesus came rapidly to the view that their founder was a unique person who had been with God since the beginning of time. This was parallel with much Jewish thought on the person of the Christ; it was held that the Christ already existed and was being held in reserve, so to speak, until God chose to send him into the world.

Then there was the doctrine of 'the suffering servant' given in the Book of Deutero-Isaiah.

'Without beauty or majesty (we saw him),
no looks to attract our eyes;
a thing despised and rejected by men,
a man of sorrows and familiar with suffering,
a man to make people screen their faces;
he was despised and we took no account of him.
And yet ours were the sufferings he bore,
ours the sorrows he carried.
But we thought of him as someone punished,
struck by God and brought low.
Yet he was pierced through for our faults,
crushed for our sins.
On him lies a punishment that brings us peace,
and through his wounds we are healed.'[2]

Clearly this passage from a prophet who can be counted
as almost the founder of Judaism is at the root of Christian
theology. While it is not certain exactly when the Disciples
of Jesus began to quote it, there can be no reasonable doubt
that they must have done so very early. It has been argued
that Jesus himself had it in mind and accordingly incurred his
own sufferings and execution. Certainly it was of high importance to the early disciples of Jesus and enabled them to state
that the crucifixion was not a disgrace but a fulfilment of
prophesy. (Actually, it is unlikely that Deutero-Isaiah meant
to refer to an individual; his 'suffering servant' was the whole
body of Jewish exiles in Babylon.) Early Christians for two
or three centuries took the passage so literally that some
taught that Jesus, in his personal appearance, had been an
ugly or even repulsive man to look at it. There is no authentic
record of what Jesus looked like and it is fascinating to
reflect that, conceivably, the tradition that he was ugly
reflected some genuine memory and was not just an interpretation of prophesy. The later Christian artistic convention
that Jesus had perfect masculine good looks is less than fully
credible; it is based upon the general theory that God would

8

be incarnate as a perfect man and upon Psalm 45: 'Of all men you are the most handsome, your lips are moist with grace.'[3] The notion of an ugly Jesus is interesting; many of the most powerful teachers and propagandists in human history have had less than perfect looks.

Deutero-Isaiah's doctrine of the suffering servant of God accepting a vicarious punishment for the sins of the world was taken whole into Christianity. To it were added a number of other Jewish details, notably those relating to 'blood', to sacrifice and to the paschal lamb.

The image of blood being shed for the benefit of the people was a common one in Jewish rabbinical thought. Some teachers held, for example, that the blood shed in the operation of circumcision had a redeeming effect. The sacrifices in the Temple represented blood being poured out before God for the benefit of the people. The story of Abraham and Isaac was a subject for much rabbinical comment. Abraham, the tradition went, had been instructed by God to make a human sacrifice of Isaac, the son he loved. Abraham obeyed, and according to rabbinical commentary Isaac was a willing victim. At the last moment, however, God stopped the killing of Isaac and provided a lamb to be sacrificed in Isaac's place. The Disciples of Jesus took over this story and adapted it to cover the crucifixion of Jesus who was the lamb sent by God to be sacrificed in the place of Isaac. (Isaac stands metaphorically for the people of God.)

In the construction of the narratives of the crucifixion of Jesus, the 'lamb' theology was an essential factor. It was held that Jesus had died upon the cross at the exact moment when the paschal lambs were being sacrificed in the Temple. To the modern generation such a coincidence might appear too good to be true but this was not how the early Christians looked at it. There is evidence that they had some difficulty in adapting real traditions to the Passover chronology. For example, there seems to have been a tradition that Jesus ate a ritual meal with his immediate followers just before he was

arrested. This meal is said in the gospels to have been the
Passover Feast but the most cursory examination shows that
it was nothing of the kind. It was held at the wrong time for
the Passover. The ordinary ritual of the Passover meal was
not followed. The Passover was a family meal which included children and women: Jesus's ceremonial meal was
for men only, although he had women followers near at hand
and had been staying with them. The natural place for a
Passover meal would have been at the house of Martha and
Mary. Jesus's last supper was not the Passover but a ritual
meal on roughly the lines of those eaten by the Essenes and
described in the Dead Sea scrolls. The gospel writers called
it the 'Passover' to make it fit their chronology but they did
not, interestingly, alter the details of it to make it fit properly.
Had they been deliberate falsifiers and forgers they could
easily have invented a proper Passover feast. The conclusion
must be that although they were writing with theological
purposes primarily in mind, and constructing a sort of
sacred drama, they did not feel free to alter authentic
material. The gospel writers were excited men wrestling with
difficult facts and theories, not liars.

One element in the sacred drama is the 'betrayal' by Judas
and this is an episode of which the meaning has been lost. As
it stands the story is incomplete and cannot be taken literally.
There is no adequate explanation of why it was necessary for
Jesus to be 'betrayed' before being executed or of what
motives could have impelled Judas. However, the surname
'Iscariot' given to Judas means 'He who delivers up' and this
suggests that Judas is a ritualistic rather than a real figure.
The impression is strengthened by Jesus being portrayed as
actually telling Judas to get on with the business of betrayal.
The roots of the story must lie in Jewish sectarian lore and
they have not yet been properly uncovered.

The accounts of the death and resurrection of Jesus appear
to have been fundamental to the Disciples of Jesus from the
beginning, although the passage of time caused them to be

interpreted ever more elaborately. Even the fixing of an authorised text of the gospels, which took at least a century (plus a further two centuries to eliminate supplementary accounts which were eventually held to be apochryphal and not correct) did not end the process. More and more details were added. The idea that Jesus had been 'nailed' to the cross crept in because Deutero-Isaiah had said 'pierced'. (There is no mention of nails in the gospels.) Ultimately the post-gospel story was rounded off with the doctrine that Jesus had been crucified on the site of the grave of Adam, from whose sin he was rescuing the human race.

Nothing points more strongly to the theological nature of the process than that the early Disciples of Jesus in Jerusalem showed an apparent total lack of interest in physical sites. Paul of Tarsus on returning from a preaching tour went to worship at the Temple and to perform his Temple duties. There is no suggestion of him visiting an empty tomb or praying at an execution site. Beyond a generalised idea that Jesus had taught in Galilee and Jerusalem and been executed at the latter, the Disciples of Jesus handed down absolutely no tradition about the sites of the events in Jesus's life. This is extraordinary in view of the wonders claimed for that life and is against ordinary human instincts. Although in the view of the present writer the weight of the evidence is that Jesus did exist as a real person, the lack of tradition about sites does arouse a nagging doubt at the back of the mind. The fact that Jerusalem was sacked by the Romans in A.D. 70 and that the early Christians were more interested in theology than in history may be a sufficient explanation. But the possibility remains that there is more to be discovered about the thought processes of the early Christians than at present meets the eye. (The present 'holy places' in Jerusalem and Bethlehem, said to be where Jesus was born, executed and resurrected, have no connection with historical tradition. Their location was determined by the dreams of a woman Roman aristocrat in the fourth century A.D., which was about as long after the event as it is now since the time of Oliver Cromwell. The need for the dreams shows that authentic tradition must have been non-existent.)

The leading characteristic of these first Disciples of Jesus was their intense spiritual excitement. They believed that they were under the immediate direction of the 'Spirit' of God, sent to them by their dead leader. The Christians still to this day celebrate the festival of Pentecost or Whitsun in commemoration of the arrival of the Spirit. In its early form it was a most dramatic doctrine which led to striking results. The Acts of the Apostles has the early Disciples of Jesus being miraculously endowed with a gift of speaking foreign languages so that they could preach to pilgrims in Jerusalem of many different nationalities. (Actually it is difficult to see why such a gift was necessary; Greek and Aramaic, between them, were enough to talk to almost anyone who came to Jerusalem.) Under the influence of the Spirit the members of the group performed miracles and guided their actions. The Spirit operated, apparently, partly through dreams, but also through direct inspiration of people while they were awake or, possibly, in a special trance. In a twentieth century context there is obviously a temptation to speculate on whether these early Christians used drugs but in fact their activity was of the same kind as Jewish prophetic inspiration and also some of the much later mediumistic activities of nineteenth and twentieth century Spiritualists. Data are lacking for any attempt at a scientific definition of what happened and, as with so much else in early Christianity, it is important to look at the whole picture rather than to attempt to rely upon any individual details within it.

However, the whole of early Christianity, including the writing of the New Testament and all the information that is available about the person and nature of Jesus sprang from people in an exalted psychological condition. They were obsessed by thoughts of signs, miracles and cosmic wonders. The result, from the point of view of scientific history, is that the full story of Jesus of Nazareth has been lost; we have only the bits of it that happened to appeal to a group which believed it was under the immediate guidance of the cosmic powers.

Who were the leaders of the Disciples of Jesus?

There is at least some reason to suppose that the chief position passed by heredity to Jesus's brother James, a devout man who, by an early account, lived austerely under a 'Nazirite' vow and prayed so much that his knees were calloused like a camel's. James is not mentioned in the gospels but in the Acts of the Apostles he is a significant figure. The conventional Christian explanation is that James only accepted his brother's teaching as a result of the resurrection; supplementary to this is the view that James was only Jesus's half-brother or a cousin, this being brought in to support the doctrine that Jesus's mother Mary was a perpetual virgin. (In the very early period, however, the doctrine of the virgin birth does not appear to have played much, if any, part, in teaching about Jesus.) Perhaps, however, James's austerity and devotion gives some clue to the type of family background from which Jesus sprang; one thinks of brothers growing up together with intense religious interests and, in adulthood, becoming religious leaders. For a hundred years, Jesus's kinsmen seem to have played a leading part in the Jesus movement at Jerusalem.

The prominence of James does not tie up with the theological significance attached to the 'Twelve', otherwise known as the 'Twelve Apostles', who were supposed to have been directly commissioned by Jesus to carry on his work and whose authority is held to have been passed down to modern Christian clergy. The activities of most of the original Twelve are obscure and the subject of legend only; there is certainly no evidence that most of them were particularly active in spreading the new faith. Their leader appears to have been the former fisherman Peter, a man of strong character, who did, apparently, work actively as a

missionary. There is sound reason to believe that eventually
he ended up as a preacher in Rome. The word 'apostle' itself
means only 'messenger' and was already in Jewish use to
describe delegates sent out from Jerusalem to the synagogues
scattered across the Mediterranean world; in the Jesus group
its use was not confined to the Twelve but was given to all
the more vigorous preachers, including such men as Paul of
Tarsus, Timothy and Barnabas who had never seen Jesus in
the flesh. Under the Twelve was a group called the 'Seven'
who apparently had some particular responsibility for the
business affairs of the group. The Seven, who later became
identified as 'deacons', all had Greek names and it has been
suggested that they were ordained in order to give Hellenistic
Jews, who existed plentifully in Jerusalem, a status in the new
sect. At one formal meeting of the group, the 'congregation'
is described as containing 120 members. All these numbers—
twelve, seven and 120—were common in Jewish mysticism;
the significance attached to them is a pointer to the minds of
the people who formed the earliest Disciples of Jesus.

In this early period the group seems to have been based on
Jerusalem, with possible satellite communities in the provincial capital Antioch (where the name 'Christians' was in
use by A.D. 43) and in Damascus. It may well have coalesced
and interacted with other Jewish groups awaiting the Christ
and feeling the inspiration of the Spirit. For example the
Damascus group may well have had an independent origin;
there is some indication that unlike the Jerusalem group it
treated its doctrines of the Christ as a secret to be revealed
only in stages to initiates sworn to confidence. Obviously,
though, Jerusalem was such a metropolitan centre, with
pilgrims continually passing through it from the rest of the
world, that such a vigorous group as the Disciples of Jesus
was bound to win an influence far beyond the city. It is easy
to suppose that within five years the germs of what became
Christianity had been carried to synagogues across the whole
Jewish diaspora; as with other sectarian ideas, they had

become an object of interest and discussion for the more religious Jews.

However, the real preaching of Christianity as the new world religion appears to have started less through the Jerusalem group than through the arrival on the scene of an independent personality, Paul of Tarsus, who claimed a personal vision of the resurrected Jesus. Paul set going a process by which within 300 years Christianity grew into the most powerful religious force in the Roman Empire.

¹ Mt 27:51–52   ² Is 53:2–5   ³ Ps 45:2

VII

The Second Founder

To turn to Paul of Tarsus after studying Jesus is to move from obscurity into the full blaze of historical certainty. It is like a motorist fumbling from a dark rural lane into an illuminated motorway. Suddenly everything becomes clear and easy. Paul was the second founder of Christianity. Any attempt to examine Jesus other than in a devotional way entails the gravest risk of getting him wrong, so incomplete are the records of him. Paul, however, is as substantial an historical character as his near contemporary Julius Caesar. Primarily this is because Paul, unlike Jesus, was a writer. He wrote long letters which are preserved to form nearly half the New Testament; anybody can read the letters and so obtain, at first hand, a sound impression of what he was like. Also the book called the 'Acts of the Apostles' is mostly the 'acts of Paul'. Scholarly disputes about Paul can be only peripheral; there is no scope for disagreement about the substance of this intelligent, exalted, dogmatic visionary.

Altogether thirteen letters ascribed to Paul have been preserved, although modern scholars have doubted the authenticity of some of them. It seems to have been the custom from the beginning to read them aloud at Christian religious meetings; the custom continues. They are the earliest part of the New Testament. They, not the gospels, are the prime authority for the bulk of Christian theory. Paul wrote the letters over a period of about twenty-five years; they range from relatively short notes to friends to such a substantial theological treatise as the Letter to the Romans.

While, doubtless, there was some element of accident in which items of his correspondence happened to be preserved and which lost, there is enough continuity and consistency in them to provide a reliable reflection of his character and mind. They are the next best thing to an autobiography.

Paul was born at the busy port of Tarsus, in what is now southern Turkey, in about A.D. 10 which would make him, according to the conventionally-accepted chronology, about fourteen years younger than Jesus. His family were Greek Jews who had, possibly, originally acquired the faith by conversion. Paul himself claimed to belong to the Israelite tribe of Benjamin but this was the kind of thing which, over the generations, could easily slip into the traditions of a convert family without it having much true significance. As can be seen in the remarkable—and inconsistent—family trees attached to Jesus at the beginnings of the gospels of Matthew and Luke, Jews of the period were more interested in symbolic than real heredity. Unlike Jesus, who seems to have belonged to fairly humble peasant stock, Paul's family belonged to the upper crust of a sophisticated city; it had the high status of Roman citizenship, which was exceptional. Most people in Tarsus would have held only local citizenship. It must be presumed, therefore, that Paul had a prosperous, cultivated upbringing. Quite probably he would have had some secular education in Greek-Roman culture but this seems to have left little mark on him, to judge by his letters. His religious education would have been in the local synagogue which, like so many others, was under the control of the Pharisee party. Long after he became a Christian, Paul proclaimed with pride: 'I am a Pharisee and the son of Pharisees.'[1] Worship and instruction in the synagogue would have been in the Greek language, the scriptures being read in the Greek Septuagint version, and it is unlikely that Paul would have picked up more than a smattering of Hebrew while a boy.

Obviously he was a highly religious youth and in his mid

'teens he left home to embark upon a prolonged course of religious study at Jerusalem, presumably with a view to becoming a rabbi. He himself specifically stated that he was a pupil of Gamaliel, grandson of Hillel and leader of the liberal wing of the Pharisees. Everything points to Paul being an intelligent, intense youth and it is easy to suppose that in addition to sitting before Gamaliel he inquired widely among other schools and sects. Presumably his studies would have included at least a visit to the monastic Essenes at Qumran who were awaiting in prayer, study and celibacy the arrival of their two Christs. the priestly one and the kingly one. Paul in his later writings attached high value to celibacy and it is tempting to suppose that he got this from the Essenes; it was not characteristic of mainstream Judaism nor, for that matter, of the earliest type of Christianity. Jesus himself, although by unanimous tradition unmarried, did not, in any of his recorded words, discuss the merits or otherwise of celibacy. Presumably his ascetic brother James, tied to his rigorously religious life by his 'Nazarene vow' was single but Peter, leader of The Twelve, is specifically stated to have been married. Paul was the man who brought Essene-type celibacy into the Christian tradition.

Paul did not meet Jesus or hear him preach. The crucifixion, at the time it happened, left him cold. If anything like the traditional chronology of Jesus is accepted, the failure of the two men to meet seems utterly extraordinary. How could Paul, aged about twenty, the eager religious student at Jerusalem, possibly have missed so exciting a teacher? There is no easy explanation. Conceivably, and this is a factor constantly to be born in mind, there was no Jesus in the sense of, or the chronology of, the gospels as traditionally understood. Another explanation, and this on balance must be regarded as the most probable, is that Jesus was simply not prominent enough to attract Paul's attention; according to the gospels, after all, the Jerusalem mission lasted only a few weeks. In other words, the failure of Paul to meet Jesus is an interesting pointer towards the obscurity of Jesus. Many other explanations have been adduced, for example that Paul was in seclusion with the Essenes during Jesus's teaching, but none of them have any basis in evidence. In his later writings, Paul himself specifically disclaimed interest in or knowledge of Jesus's life as a Galilean prophet. Paul was interested only in the mystical Jesus whom he saw in visions. 'The only knowledge that I claimed to know was about Jesus', he wrote, 'and only about him as the crucified Christ.'[2]

What were Paul's views before he was converted by a vision into becoming a follower of the crucified Jesus?

He himself is silent on the subject except in the negative sense that he opposed the early Jesus-followers. The tendency has been to write of him as a devout Pharisee, trying to find happiness in the ever more meticulous observance of Jewish ritual rules: his discovery of Jesus liberated him from this dull existence. Certainly it can be taken that Paul was a Pharisee in that he believed in personal contact between God and the individual believer, in demons and angels and in the resurrection of the dead. But, in addition, he seems to have been excited by the more mystical type of Judaism and by the occult. He mentions one mystical experience in which he was lifted up into 'the third heaven' which means, presumably, that he accepted the occult Jewish teaching current in his day that there were a series of different heavens—the rabbis of this type distinguished seven heavens and a few of them claimed experiences similar to that mentioned by Paul. As a Christian preacher, Paul claimed that he had a direct and special mission from God, that he had been chosen for the work while still in his mother's womb. He said that he no longer lived as Paul but only as Christ in Paul. Such statements indicate that he was a man haunted by a sense of destiny and it is easy to suppose that in his pre-Christian period he already had some sense of having been especially chosen by God; conceivably, even, he may have suspected that he himself was to be the Christ. Many Christian writers have characterised him before his conversion as a stiff formalist, interested only in the technicalities of Jewish religious observance, but this is almost certainly incorrect. Paul was a warm man, a mystic, an enthusiast and there was plenty of scope for such qualities in first century Judaism. If in nothing else, he showed hot zeal in persecuting the first Christians.

In Paul one is dealing with that rare type of individual who crops up over the centuries with visions that he is capable of making other people believe really happened. All religions, including even twentieth century Judaism, occasionally throw them up. The nearest parallel to Paul is the prophet Mahomet who constructed the religion of Islam on the basis of his visions. An even more interesting figure is the American Joseph Smith who in 1830 founded the Church of Jesus Christ of Latter Day Saints (the Mormons), a body which is powerful and still growing. Although there are some obscurities in Smith's career and his personal integrity is questioned by some, he stands uniquely as a prophet who founded a lasting new religion in the days of newspapers and railroads. He can be studied in a way that Mahomet and Paul cannot.

Smith experienced his basic visions during the 1820s, when he said he saw God the Father with Jesus Christ and received the 'Book of Mormon' from an angel. From time to time during the rest of his life he announced further revelations which had come to him. He built Mormonism upon Christianity in much the same manner as Christianity is built upon Judaism. Smith possessed high talents of leadership and oratory; also he seems to have been capable of literally hypnotising people and to have been a faith-healer. The fascinating parallel with early Christianity is the intense antagonism aroused, for no very clear reason, by the early Mormon community. (It had nothing to do with Mormon plural marriage, which was a later development.) Because of their doctrines, Smith and his followers were persecuted in a

manner unique in American religious history—they were
beaten up, tarred and feathered, driven from their farms and
murdered. One massacre, involving Mormon men, women
and children was carried out with the connivance of the
Missouri state authorities. Smith himself died at the hands
of a semi-official lynching party which got him while he was
in gaol. To look at early Mormon history is to get in a
modern and well-reported context a glimmering of the furies
a new religion can arouse and, also, of how martyrdom can
strengthen a faith. To say that the American Christians, as an
organised body, were responsible for massacring Mormons is
on a par with saying that 'the Jews' were responsible for the
sufferings of Jesus and some of the early Christians. It is
unreasonable to smear a community as a whole for the
actions of some members of it.

To place Paul, Mahomet, Smith, or for that matter
Deutero-Isaiah, in the same category is not to pass judgment
on the authenticity or quality of their doctrines. It can be
observed only that they all belong to the rare but identifiable
type of men whose visionary experiences are a solid force
in history. They are different from Jesus or the Buddha
in neither of whose lives do visions appear to have been
of central importance and who taught on their own
authority.

Paul's first contacts with the Jerusalem Church seem to
have come when he was aged in his mid-twenties and his
reaction was one of bitter distaste. Jesus had then been dead
for about six years (accepting the customary chronology)
but the Jerusalem Church was thriving on the doctrine that
he had risen from the dead and was due to return as the
Messiah. Paul who had his own esoteric interests in this kind
of thing believed that they had got the whole thing blas-
phemously wrong and he began to play a leading part in
persecuting them. He took part in the semi-official stoning of
one of their leaders, the deacon Stephen (the circumstances
are strikingly similar to those of Joseph Smith in that a man

in legal custody was killed), and obtained some kind of official commission to arrest members of the group. Paul's zeal and bitterness are not easy to explain. They were certainly not characteristic of the Pharasaical party as a whole; his own former teacher, Gamaliel, is specifically quoted as saying of the Jerusalem Church: 'Leave these men alone and let them go. If this enterprise, this movement of theirs, is of human origin it will break up of its own accord; but if it does in fact come from God you will not only be unable to destroy them, but you might find yourselves fighting against God.'[3] In persecuting the Jerusalem Church, Paul was associating with the conservative Sadducee party which detested 'enthusiasm' and talk of the Christ as politically dangerous; it was an odd posture for a man who was himself an 'enthusiast' in such matters. It reflects, perhaps, Paul's vigorous nature and sense of mission. He was affronted that this group was making claims that seemed inconsistent with his own studies and his own destiny. Probably, too, he was undergoing the psychological process, not unknown in love between the sexes, of repulsion being the preliminary to fascination.

In the winter of A.D. 36–37 Paul set off on some kind of a mission to persecute a Messianic group at Damascus which was either a branch of the Jerusalem Church or was closely associated with it. Somewhere on the road he experienced a vision which changed his life and which can be accounted the origin of Christianity as a new world religion. Accounts of the vision differ in one or two details but in substance they are the same. At midday he felt a bright light around him and he fell to the ground. He heard a voice which said: 'Saul, Saul, why are you persecuting me?' He replied: 'Who are you, Lord?' The voice said: 'I am Jesus and you are persecuting me.'[4] Whether or not Paul believed that he saw Jesus, as well as heard him, at this moment is not clear. He certainly claimed later that he had seen Jesus but he may have been referring to some occasion subsequent to the Damascus road experience.

His immediate behaviour was not that of an ordinary convert to a new religion. He did not seek a course of instruction from existing members of the faith. He evinced no thirst for information about the life and work of Jesus of Nazareth. Instead he went off in solitary meditation. The Acts of the Apostles does portray him going into Damascus, making contact with a disciple of Jesus and getting baptised — Straight Street, where this is said to have happened, still exists — but Paul himself, in his letter to the Galatians gives a different story: '. . . God, who had specially chosen me while I was still in my mother's womb, called me through his grace and chose to reveal his Son in me, so that I might preach the Good News about him to the pagans. I did not stop to discuss this with any human being, nor did I go up to Jerusalem to see those who were already apostles before me, but I went off to Arabia at once and later went straight back from there to Damascus. Even when after three years I went up to Jerusalem to visit Cephas [Peter] and stayed with him for fifteen days, I did not see any of the other apostles; I only saw James, the brother of the Lord, and I swear before God that what I have just written is the literal truth.'[5]

Paul's version, presumably, must be taken as correct. He is writing with much vehemence on a matter on which only he could have first hand knowledge. 'Arabia', to which he went, must mean what is now the Kingdom of Jordan, a relatively empty area with plenty of desert places attractive to a man who wanted to go into solitary meditation. There, presumably, he worked out the rest of his mission, by straightforward pondering or further visions, or both, and decided that his life's work must be to preach Jesus as the Christ. (The original Damascus road vision gave him no specific injunction to preach; had it done so, the fact is likely to have been recorded.) Only after he had worked out his theology — and the process may have taken him as long as three years — did he make contact with the Jerusalem leaders.

Indirect evidence of Paul's lack of contact with the Jerusalem Church and of his disinterest in Jesus's life can be gathered from his writings. Assuming that the mainstream tradition of Jesus be substantially correct, Paul was converted only about eight years after Jesus had finished his public teaching. Although the gospels were not yet written, there must have been masses of oral information available from people who had known Jesus, heard him and even lived with him. Nowhere in Paul's writings is there any mention of such material. He quotes not a single parable of Jesus's, not a single word of Jesus's teaching, not a single miracle. Even when he sets out the procedure for the ritual meal of bread and wine, he says he does so on visionary authority — 'This is what I received from the Lord.'[6] Paul's interest in Jesus was solely in the mystical Christ who had appeared in his visions and who, he believed, was shortly to come down from heaven in glory. 'I have seen the Lord', he affirmed, and he equated his own experience of a resurrected Jesus exactly with the experiences of the original followers immediately after the crucifixion.[7] (This, incidentally, is one of the more useful pointers to the nature of the resurrection.) While it would be unreasonable to treat Paul's letters as if they were a systematic religious thesis they must be taken as at least a rough reflection of his preaching and doctrine. Had he been quoting Jesus's words as an ordinary preacher does, this would surely have been at least dimly evident in his letters.

So far as can be ascertained, Paul stood head and shoulders above everyone else as the propagator of the new faith. He had a dynamic urge to convert men to his way of thinking. That Paul was so prominent so early in the history of Christianity is itself a curiosity and not the obvious way a religion might be expected to spread. The Buddha, after a lifetime of teaching, left a band of disciples who had known him well and were his natural successors in leadership. Mahomet passed on the leadership to his own family. There are some traces of these obvious kinds of arrangements being attempted in Christianity. The gospels, notably Matthew and Mark, have Jesus selecting a special group of twelve disciples (reduced to eleven by the defection of Judas) and specifically commissioning them, after the resurrection, to found a new world religion. 'Go, therefore, make disciples of all nations.'[8] Leaving aside the point that post-resurrection utterances must be regarded as revelations and not ordinary human communication, there is no historical evidence, save possibly in the case of Peter, that the eleven did anything of the kind. The careers of all of them are known in legend only. The missionary whose life-work was considered worth preserving in written form in some detail was Paul, who had never met his near contemporary Jesus save in visions. There are also some Mahomet-like traces of the leadership in early Christianity being passed down through members of the founder's family. This would have been in accord with Pharisaical Judaism in which the Hillel-Gamaliel dynasty was allowed hereditary authority. James, the brother of Jesus, is represented as the leader at Jerusalem and there is evidence, of moderate soundness, that the Jesus dynasty continued in authority there for about a century; however there is no sign of the family being engaged in spreading the faith beyond Palestine. Paul, who claimed a direct commission from the resurrected Jesus 'that I might preach the Good News about him to the pagans',[9] was the effective founder of Christianity as a world religion.

From Paul's writings one gets an impression of an autocratic man whose powers of persuasion rested on straightforward, vivid assertion rather than upon tricks of propaganda. There are no intriguing twists in Paul's teachings to beguile the mind, as in the parables of Jesus, but just dogmas thundered out. He was possibly not a particularly likeable man, being too assertive to be a comfortable companion; his friends were his subordinates rather than his equals. There exists a physical description of him which is certainly very old and may well be authentic; indeed it is the only physical description of a New Testament personality of any historical value at all. According to it, he was a far from prepossessing figure. There was nothing of the Dr. Billy Graham about his looks. He was short, slightly bow-legged, bald, bearded, and had a prominent nose with eyebrows joining above it. He suffered from some kind of ailment which, he wrote, made him 'repulsive'. Could it have been a skin disease? Perhaps, though, he had some form of personal charm. Advising Christians on how to influence non-believers, he wrote: 'Talk to them agreeably and with a flavour of wit, and try to fit your answers to the needs of each one.'[10]

Paul made three missionary journeys around the eastern Mediterranean, principally in what is now Turkey, and the evidence ends with him a prisoner in Rome. There is a possibility that he made a fourth missionary journey westwards from Rome, taking in Spain and, conceivably, even Britain. His supposed landing place in Britain is Paulsgrove, near Portsmouth, but the traditions attached to Paulsgrove are extremely late and the correct derivation of the name is probably 'pale', meaning a fence. However it can be said for the Paulsgrove theory that it is next to what was a big Roman settlement at Porchester and thus a plausible landing place. What is certainly true about Paul's travels is that plenty of facilities were available both by road and by sea anywhere within the Roman Empire and, for that matter, beyond it eastwards on the caravan routes to India and China. If one could not exactly buy a ticket to get from Jerusalem to London in those days, one could plan the journey with a reasonable assurance of completing it and of how long it would take and how much it would cost. Communications were not so good again until the nineteenth century. Paul seems to have financed himself—in his letters he takes pride that he is never a burden on his converts. His Roman citizenship indicates a well-to-do family and so quite probably he had some fortune of his own. In addition he seems sometimes to have worked at the craft of a tentmaker, sewing at night and preaching by day; this was thoroughly within the Jewish custom of that time by which, at least in theory, every rabbi was supposed to earn a living and give his religious services free. That travel was easy does not mean that it was necessarily comfortable, especially at sea; the Acts of the Apostles contains a dramatic account of Paul being shipwrecked.

The title adopted by Paul and his associates, and also given to the Twelve, was that of 'apostle'. This means 'messenger' and it was already in use among the Jews. Apostles went out from the Temple at Jerusalem to teach in distant synagogues, to collect money and to regulate feasts and discipline. Paul specifically stated that his commission as an apostle came not from the Jerusalem group but directly from his vision of Jesus. The wonder is not that he sometimes clashed with the original group but that it accepted him at all; a prophet appearing in modern Rome, claiming to possess new doctrines directly vouchsafed to him by Jesus, would not command the immediate adherence of the Vatican. However, control was loose and Paul abroad on his missions seems to have been cut off altogether from the Jerusalem group for most of the time.

Paul's essential base of operations was the Jewish synagogues which existed in every city, at least of the eastern Roman Empire. They were vigorous places with much religious devotion and also debate on the purposes of God. To portray them, as some Christian writers have done, as dry or formal is to miss the central point that Judaism was a religion of argument. Of a world community of about four million Jews, about half lived outside Palestine. Obviously the directly political movements which existed among many of the Palestinian Jews could have no counterpart in the dispersion; any Jew who felt really strongly about fighting for an independent Jewish state would go to Palestine to do so. Similarly a dispersed Jew who was deeply interested in the Hebrew roots of his religion might go to the great rabbinical schools at Jerusalem, as Paul himself had done. But the mainstream of the dispersed Jews were content to live as a minority among pagans. They maintained vigorous communal institutions and sought to influence and convert the pagans around them, but accepted the Roman political framework, which allowed them privileges and exemptions which made the practice of their faith possible. In Alexandria, which was almost as important a Jewish centre as Jerusalem itself, the philosopher Philo, a near-contemporary of Jesus and Paul, was preaching a sober reconciliation between Judaism and Greek philosophy. The Jewish scriptures, he taught, contained a divine revelation which, if it were not handled extravagantly, could be married to the best of pagan philosophy to form a universal religion. Within a century Philo's ideas were to be influential among the Christians, but Paul belonged to a radically different Jewish tendency, that of the Messianic enthusiasts from Palestine. Paul was not interested in the cool reconciliation of Judaism with Hellenism but only in preaching the Christ.

Of course it is difficult to be precise about figures but it is likely that Paul's converts were numbered only in thousands, or at the most tens of thousands. He was only a peripheral force in the massive Jewish world community. As can clearly be detected in the New Testament, he was only one of many teachers of various types who were taking to the dispersed Jews the excitements of the Messianic doctrines in the Holy Land. It is important not to get him larger than life. Philo was much better known than he was. Moreover, Paul's activities were overshadowed by the events surrounding the Jewish rebellion in Palestine in A.D. 66, which was a religious as well as a political affair. The boiling up of Jewish enthusiasts towards this rebellion was an infinitely more prominent current in the Jewish world than the rise of Christianity.

Paul's ordinary method on arriving at a fresh city was to address the local synagogue. He said the Christ had already appeared briefly on earth but had been crucified, that he, Paul, had had a vision of Jesus, and that Jesus was about to reappear in glory and the dead resurrected. He called on the members to be baptized in Jesus's name and thus to share in the new covenant between God and the chosen people. That Paul was able, without particular difficulty, to get talking to synagogues on such lines is itself an indication of the nature of the Judaism of the time. It would be difficult to imagine a modern orthodox synagogue allowing such a teacher into its official pulpit. In Paul's day, though, it seems to have been normal to allow any visiting teacher, especially one who had studied at Jerusalem, to give his views an airing. It was a part of the tradition of debate. Not surprisingly, most Jews refused to accept Paul's teaching; apart from anything else, his doctrine of the Christ was far from obviously in line with Jewish scripture and tradition. When he insisted on going on and on about Jesus, he was barred from the official pulpit but meanwhile he had gained a few converts who continued to meet under his leadership in private houses. Doubtless the same kind of thing was happening with other Jewish sectarian teachers. The process was accompanied by a certain amount of heat, and sometimes even violence; believers in the Pauline doctrine accused the Jewish majority of 'rejecting the Christ', while the Jewish majority accused Paul of debasing and dividing their religion. In retrospect, however, it can be reckoned that both sides were acting reasonably according to their beliefs and consciences.

The category with which Paul seems to have been most successful was that of the 'God-fearers', that is people who attended synagogue services without being full members of the Jewish community. They were numerous, perhaps in some places outnumbering the full Jews, and they had a recognised place in the Jewish system. Some rabbis taught that it was the eventual Jewish mission to convert all mankind into God-fearers, the Jews themselves being a kind of hereditary priesthood to serve everyone else. Deutero-Isaiah had dramatically described Jerusalem as the future capital of the world: 'Your gates will lie open continually, shut neither by day nor by night, for men to bring you the wealth of the nations with their kings leading them.'[11] Of course it was possible for an outsider to become a full Jew, and this did quite often happen, but it involved acceptance of the detailed Jewish way of life laid down in the Torah and also, for men, the uncomfortable operation of circumcision. The easier way was to be just a God-fearer, which involved only the following of basic moral laws and abstention from meat which had been offered to idols.

Since the God-fearers were less deeply rooted in Jewish tradition than were the full Jews, it is easy to imagine so vivid a teacher as Paul making an impression on them. In addition, once he had got his own group going, Paul seems to have attracted converts direct from paganism and who had not been attached to the synagogue at all.

Then Paul took the crucial decision that anybody who had been baptized in the name of Jesus counted as a full member of the House of Israel. In other words, his converts instead of being in the second-class status of God-fearers were promoted to first-class rank.

Obviously this decision was the birth of Christianity as a separate religion from Judaism but the point is clear only in retrospect; Paul was interested in getting Judaism on to what he considered the right lines, not in breaking away from it. Paul lived and died a Jew in much the same way as John Wesley, founder of Methodism, lived and died an Anglican. In retrospect it is plain, too, that the decision was of fundamental importance in making Christianity attractive to a wide public. The success of the synagogues in attracting God-fearers demonstrated that there was a hunger for Jewish-type monotheism and that the Jewish scriptures were capable of exerting a wide appeal. However, the second-class status of the God-fearers was inherently unattractive while to become a full Jew was a difficult and even alien process.

Paul offered full status on terms easily acceptable by a pagan. But this was more important for the future than in Paul's own day; at least up to the revolt of A.D. 66, mainstream Judaism was probably attracting many more converts than was the infant Christian sect.

Up to this stage, Christianity had been an esoteric inner sect of Judaism. One could no more become a Christian without first being a Jew than today one could become a Trappist without first being a Roman Catholic. Paul's throwing the thing wide open seems to have caused the most severe strains, which are plainly reflected in the New Testament. The details are far from plain but it does seem that rival apostles were sent out from Jerusalem to contradict Paul's teachings. There was also some kind of council, attended by Paul at Jerusalem — it must be remembered that Paul and the Jerusalem followers of Jesus hardly knew each other. The evidence is lacking to describe what happened with any historical reliability but certainly in the long run the Pauline teaching triumphed.

The great enigma is the figure of Peter of Galilee, the leading personality of the Twelve. A considerable theology was to be erected around him and in the gospels, which reached their final form after both he and Paul were dead, he is represented as an impetuous fisherman who was given a special commission by Jesus. One, extreme, view of him is that he was a ritualistic rather than a real figure and that the name Peter is a code-word for an Essene overseer. Exactly opposed to this is the mainstream Christian tradition that he was an active teacher and leader who ended by being crucified in Rome; certainly from very near the beginning, the bishops of Rome were claiming a special authority on the ground that they were successors of Peter. The mainstream tradition could be correct but the sparsity of evidence for it is nearly as tantalising as the sparsity of evidence about Jesus himself. There are two short letters attributed to Peter in the New Testament but there is nothing remarkable about them and they follow the same general line of doctrine as Paul's much longer and more abundant letters. They seem to have been written when Christianity had already been established for some decades and people were beginning to wonder why the Christ had not returned yet. '. . . With the Lord "a day" can mean a thousand years, and a thousand years is like a day. The Lord is not being slow to carry out his promises, as anybody else might be called slow; but he is being patient with you all, wanting nobody to be lost and everybody to be brought to change his ways. The Day of the Lord will come like a thief, and then with a roar the sky will vanish, the elements will catch fire and fall apart, the earth and all that it contains will be burnt up.'[12]

Obviously it was a difficulty, felt even during the period of the composition of the New Testament, that whereas Peter, ritualistically, was supposed to be the chief apostle and had received direct authority from Jesus, in practice the leading preacher and maker of doctrine was Paul. The solution has been to bring the two men as closely as possible together. To this day it is the Roman Catholic custom to have an altar to St. Paul in any church dedicated to St. Peter, and an altar to St. Peter in any church dedicated to St. Paul.

Paul's teaching was practical and exciting, forecasting the most vivid supernatural events about to take place. He really believed, and got his converts to believe also, that the world was about to come to an end. Believers would fly up into the sky to meet the returning Christ, dead believers leaping from their graves for the purpose. 'Any of us who are left alive until the Lord's coming', he wrote, 'will not have any advantage over those who have died. At the trumpet of God, the voice of the archangel will call out the command and the Lord himself will come down from heaven; those who have died in Christ will be the first to rise, and then those of us who are still alive will be taken up in the clouds, together with them, to meet the Lord in the air.'[13] This is strong doctrine and readily comprehensible. As a foretaste of what was to come,

Paul's converts experienced what they called 'the gifts of the Spirit'. Leading personalities among them fell into trances and spoke in 'tongues', that is unknown languages; others gave out prophetic utterances and described visions they had seen. Paul welcomed this but obviously had difficulty in keeping it under control. His own credentials, after all, were based upon visions and in case of conflict between his visions and another man's he had only the force of his personality to make his own prevail. On some occasions, at least, he failed to prevail and rival prophets got control of his communities. Exactly what went on is impossible to reconstruct; even at the time an informed reporter would have had difficulty in making coherent the complicated and rival currents within early Christianity. The enormous strength of Paul was his breadth of vision. It would be easy today to dismiss him as an obsolete crank who believed funny things about angels and demons and the imminent resurrection of the dead. Then, in reading him, one comes across the occasional passage of universal and timeless significance.

'If I have all the eloquence of men or of angels, but speak without love, I am simply a gong booming or a cymbal clashing. If I have the gift of prophecy, understanding all the mysteries there are, and knowing everything, and if I have faith in all its fulness, to move mountains, but without love, then I am nothing at all. If I give away all that I possess, piece by piece, and if I even let them take my body to burn it, but am without love, it will do me no good whatever . . . Love does not come to an end. But if there are gifts of prophecy, the time will come when they must fail; or the gift of languages, it will not continue for ever; and knowledge— for this, too, the time will come when it must fail. For our knowledge is imperfect and our prophesying is imperfect; but once perfection comes, all imperfect things will disappear. When I was a child, I used to talk like a child, and think like a child, and argue like a child, but now I am a man, all childish ways are put behind me. Now we are seeing but a dim reflection in a mirror; but then we shall be seeing face to face. The knowledge that I have now is imperfect; but then I shall know as fully as I am known. In short, there are three things that last; faith, hope and love; and the greatest of these is love.'[14]

Unless the force of such passages is absorbed, it is impossible to understand why Christianity became the largest world religion.

There is also a universality in much of Paul's purely moral advice. It follows closely the ideas of Jesus and, also, of the mainstream Jewish rabbis. But Paul always expresses it in his own words. He does not quote even the Sermon on the Mount, with its extraordinary 'love your enemies' injunction, but gives his own equivalent: 'Bless those who persecute you; never curse them, bless them. Rejoice with those who rejoice and be sad with those in sorrow. Treat everyone with equal kindness; never be condescending but make real friends with the poor. Do not allow yourself to become self-satisfied. Never repay evil with evil but let everyone see you are interested only in the highest ideals. Do all you can to live at peace with everyone. Never try to get revenge; leave that, my friends, to God's anger.'[15]

The extent to which Paul's converts needed moral advice is not clear. On the one hand they were exalted people who were expecting the Christ to return at any moment. One would expect them to have no taste for gross sins. On the other hand, they had been let into the House of Israel on easy terms and were subject to none of the normal Jewish discipline. Might they not practice pagan habits which, especially in sexual matters, were repugnant to Judaism? Paul in his letters rails at what he considered misconduct among his converts, but he may well have just been easily shocked. It would be unreasonable, however, to represent him as being excessively puritanical or anti-sex. He followed the normal Jewish line that sex should be contained within a stable married life. 'It is a good thing for a man not to touch a woman,' he wrote, 'but since sex is always a danger, let each man have his own wife and each woman her own husband. The husband must give his wife what she has the right to expect, and so too the wife to the husband. The wife has no rights over her own body; it is the husband who has them. In the same way, the husband has no rights over his body; the wife has them. Do not refuse each other except by mutual consent, and then only for an agreed time, to leave yourselves free for prayer; then come together again lest Satan should take advantage of your weakness to tempt you . . . There is something I want to add for the sake of widows and those who are not married; it is a good thing for them to stay as they are, like me, but if they cannot control the sexual urges, they should get married, since it is better to be married than to be tortured.'[16] Paul permitted divorce in some cases of a believer married to a non-believer, a provision which remains in Roman Catholic canon law. He made no mention of artificial contraception, techniques of which were used in his time.

It is sometimes held that Paul's personal celibacy put him outside the Jewish tradition, which in its mainstream form is based primarily on the family, but this hardly stands up against the fact of the Essene celibacy which existed in his time. The ancient Jewish patriarchs, Abraham, Isaac and Jacob are represented as family men, proud of their wives and their wealth, but one wonders whether this kind of thing applied to all the later prophets. One would not be too surprised to discover that Deutero-Isaiah, whoever he was, remained a virgin. Whatever psychological explanation may be adduced, it remains a fact of life that some people are so absorbed by religion that they do without sex. Paul was more moderate than the Buddha, who taught that celibacy was essential for the maximum religious development. It has also been held that Paul was anti-woman. Certainly he enjoined wives to be submissive to their husbands and daughters to their fathers and was opposed to women speaking at religious meetings. However such views were normal in his time save, perhaps, in certain upper class Roman families. To this day in orthodox Jewish synagogues the men and women sit apart. It is absurd to blame Paul for not holding particular views about women which have become current in Europe only in the last two generations, and incorrect to ascribe to him the the sole responsibility for the puritanical strain which has always existed in Christianity. While Jesus's views on such subjects are not recorded in any detail, it is overwhelmingly probable that they were the same as Paul's, or, come to that, the same as Gamaliel's. Paul brought in a balancing factor; a wife was to obey her husband but he in return, he said, should love her as much as the Christ loved the Church. The references to individual women in his letters indicate that his preaching was at least as effective with females as with males.

Where Paul broke new ground was not in his morals but in his doctrine. Above all, he introduced what became the central Christian doctrine of the atonement. This was that the crucifixion of Jesus was not a mere misadventure but a central part of God's arrangements for the world. Jesus had suffered to make up for men's sins. For historical purposes it is tantalising, even infuriating, that Paul in his letters takes such a completely ritualistic view of the crucifixion. Apart from a single reference to it having happened under Pontius Pilate, he gives no account of how or why it happened, the form of the trial, the time of year or the place of burial. Either he did not know at all or else he considered such details unimportant. Since his letters were the earliest part of the New Testament to be written, the gap is serious. By the time, the gospel accounts were written a generation later, the atonement theory had already obtained its hold and this makes highly suspect their accounts that Jesus died during the Seder festival at exactly the moment the paschal lambs were being sacrificed in the Temple. Just a sentence in Paul about what really happened would clarify enormous historical problems.

The condition for benefiting from Jesus's sacrifice was to

believe in him. 'If your lips confess that Jesus is Lord and if
you believe in your heart that God raised him from the dead,
then you will be saved,'[17] Paul wrote. People who refused to
believe or were unable to believe would suffer. 'He will come
in flaming fire to impose the penalty on all who do not
acknowledge God and refuse to accept the Lord Jesus. It will
be their punishment to be lost eternally.'[18] Paul avoided,
however, any detailed discussion of heaven, hell or purgatory
such as was common in later Christianity. The central point
was that the Christ was about to change everything. 'The
world as we know it is passing away,'[19] he wrote.

What Paul did not teach was that Jesus was God. Any such
idea was impossible for any Jew; above all the contending
sects in the Judaism of the time, the central doctrine of the
single, invisible God stood absolutely sacrosanct. There is just
one passage in the Pauline letters which implies that Jesus
was divine, but this is almost certainly a later interpolation;
it is in the form of a short hymn which somebody put into
the text. Beyond doubt, if Paul *had* believed in the divinity of
Jesus, his letters would have been full of it; nothing to him
could have been more exciting. But Paul, following the
ordinary Jewish line of thought on the Christ, held that Jesus
was a uniquely privileged person, the elder brother of all
mankind, the second Adam, God's deputy but still, in the
last resort, the creation of God. From the evidence of Paul's
letters, it must be taken that the idea that Jesus was God
made man dated from a later period. It begins to emerge in
the gospel of John, written at the end of the first century,
about thirty-five years after Paul's death. Incidentally,
Paul makes no mention of any special form of birth for
Jesus.

Paul's letters are the most readable and most impressive
part of the New Testament. This is because they are the first-
hand words of a real person. The gospels have their own
appeal for the reader willing to guess about the elusive personality of Jesus of Nazareth but the obscurities are such as

to make them readable as history only by a scholar equipped with technical knowledge. (Their devotional or inspirational impact is another matter.) With Paul's letters there are few technical difficulties and anyone who knows Greek can read them exactly as they came from him. He dictated them to a secretary to fit circumstances which are easily identifiable and, usually, at the end added a note in his own writing. Their swift changes in mood and pace convey an impression of Paul in action. At one moment he is at his grandest: 'There is only one mediator between God and mankind, himself a man, Christ Jesus.'[20] Then a few lines later in the same letter he is giving intimate advice to a friend: 'You should give up drinking only water and have a little wine for the sake of your digestion and the frequent bouts of illness that you have.'[21] The conventional New Testament arrangement of the letters, by their length, is useless. They should be read in the order in which they were written, which is: First and Second Thessalonians, First and Second Corinthians, Galatians, Romans, Philippians, Ephesians, Colossians, Philemon, First Timothy, Titus, Second Timothy. (The last three have been strongly challenged on their authenticity as Pauline writings.) The Epistle to the Hebrews, although possibly based upon Paul's thought, was written by some unknown author in a literary style which is different from Paul's; doubts about the authorship of it have existed since very early days.

The last four letters were addressed to personal friends but the others were specifically written to be read aloud to Christian groups. Although, obviously, Paul does not describe the nature of the groups — that would already have been well-known to the members — it is possible to deduce certain facts about them. They were meeting in independence, or semi-independence, of the mainstream Jewish synagogal organisation, and were adopting the name of 'churches'. The members called themselves saints, that is holy ones, and included both sexes. There were the beginnings of a professional priesthood, some of the senior men members holding positions of leadership and presiding at services; presumably they held some sort of authority from Paul or other apostles and this seems to have been conferred by a laying on of hands.

Old translations of the New Testament, including the Authorised Version, have a letter in Paul's name referring to the office of 'bishop' but this did not mean a bishop in anything approaching the modern sense of a man ordained to supervise a large number of Christian communities. A bishop to Paul meant the senior member of a local church and, indeed, the best translation of his words is not bishop but 'presiding elder' or 'president'. The letter lays down the qualifications for such a person. 'To want to be a presiding elder is to want to do noble work. That is why the president must have an impeccable character. He must not have been married more than once, and he must be temperate, discreet and courteous, hospitable and a good teacher; not a heavy drinker nor hot-tempered, but kind and peaceable. He must not be a lover of money. He must be a man who manages his own family well and brings his children up to obey him and be well-behaved; how can any man who does not understand how to manage his own family have responsibility for the church of God? He should not be a new convert, in case pride might turn his head and then he might be condemned as the devil was condemned. It is also necessary that people outside the Church should speak well of him, so that he never gets a bad reputation and falls into the devil's trap.'[22] This was written in about A.D. 65 when Paul had been preaching for nearly thirty years; it indicates that the new system had begun to settle down and become self-propagating, there being no need to give high office to new converts.

From the qualifications for president Paul passes straight on the qualifications for the junior leaders, the deacons. Exactly what the deacons were supposed to do is not clear but, presumably, they assisted the president and probably also looked after the local church's charitable and pastoral affairs: they seem to have included members of both sexes. 'Deacons', says the same letter, 'must be respectable men whose word can be trusted, moderate in the amount of wine they drink and with no squalid greed for money. They must be conscientious believers in the mystery of the faith. They are to be examined first, and only admitted to serve as deacons if there is nothing against them. In the same way, the women must be respectable, not gossips but sober and quite reliable. Deacons must not have been married more than once, and must be men who manage their children and families well.'[23]

Further on the same letter refers to 'elders'. It is not clear whether they were identical with the president or an intermediate rank between president and deacon; in all probability the customs varied in different churches. The letter contemplates them being paid for their services. 'The elders who do their work well while they are in charge are to be given double consideration, especially those who are assiduous in preaching and teaching. As scripture says: You must not muzzle an ox when it is treading out corn; and again: The worker deserves his pay. Never accept any accusation brought against an elder unless it is supported by two or three witnesses. If any of them are at fault, reprimand them publicly as a warning to the rest.'[24]

The main ritual of the communities was a ceremonial meal. Paul criticises a custom at Corinth by which the members brought their own food as at a picnic but without sharing it out. 'When the time comes to eat', wrote Paul, 'everyone is in such a hurry to start his own supper that one person goes hungry while another is getting drunk. Surely you have homes for eating and drinking in? Surely you have enough respect for the community of God not to make poor people embarrassed?'[25] Paul insisted on the symbolic importance of bread and wine as the body and blood of the Christ. 'Everyone is to recollect himself before eating this bread and drinking this cup; because a person who eats and drinks without recognising the Body is eating and drinking his own

10

condemnation. In fact that is why many of you are weak and ill and some have died. If only we recollected ourselves, we should not be punished like that ... To sum up, my dear brothers, when you meet for the Meal, wait for one another. Anyone who is hungry should eat at home, and then your meeting will not bring your condemnation.'[26] This passage would seem to indicate confusion among the early Christians about how to run the ceremonial meal they had taken over from the Essenes and, indeed, from Judaism generally. Paul obviously was pressing for something approaching the modern Holy Communion and the authority he claimed was direct from Jesus but the tradition of the Communion being within the framework of a full meal subsisted, in some places, for up to six centuries. For at least the first century of Christianity it is impossible reliably to disentangle 'Holy Communion' from the wider 'love feast'.

The modern Christian Church can reasonably claim an uninterrupted descent from the groups to which Paul addressed his letters. In the broadest outline, the distinguishing marks of modern Christianity were already there—admission to anyone on baptism, the ceremonial meal, ordained leaders, faith that Jesus's execution was an atonement for the sins of mankind. The fundamental revolution against the original Disciples of Jesus at Jerusalem had already taken place; with their Temple worship, their devout practice of the Jewish Torah, their sharing of property, their leadership by kin of the founder, the Jerusalem disciples are alien to modern Christianity in a way that the Pauline groups are not. To point to a direct descent of modern Christianity from the Pauline groups is not, however, to say that the two things are identical. About 1,500 years afterwards there was some attempt in the European Protestant Reformation to seek out a 'primitive' Christianity that would be purer than the medieval Catholic Church. The attempt was a delusion in any historical (as opposed, possibly, to a devotional) sense. One can go back and back through the centuries in search of

Christianity in a less developed form but it is difficult to pin down any point at which things were obviously perfect; if one goes back and back, one does not know where to stop and eventually arrives at a purely Jewish sect. Pauline Christianity would be unattractive if it were reintroduced in the twentieth century and, anyway, the data is lacking from which an accurate copy could be made. The Pauline Christians were dynamic, superstitious, and eagerly awaiting the return of the Christ and the resurrection of the dead. They trusted dreams, visions and unknown tongues. Their forms of organisation probably had little consistency and there were many quarrels. They did not believe that Jesus was God, or, at most, they were only just beginning to feel their way towards such a belief. They had no gospels and relied upon word of mouth for stories about the life of Jesus; doubtless some of the stories were rather wild. They were the germ of modern Christianity, in its various forms, but there is no historical reason for supposing that any particular modern Christian group has more identity than any other with the Paulines. Protestantism, when it eventually came, was something new and not, as it wanted to be, a true return to the past. Argument about the true heirs of the Paulines is as profitless, in political terms, as it would be to argue whether Richard Nixon or Hubert Humphrey was the true heir of George Washington.

From the beginning, Christianity attracted a degree of persecution. Whether this was primarily for 'political' or 'religious' reasons is difficult to disentangle and, anyway, it was not the kind of distinction that many made at that time. The Roman Empire itself was a religious organisation, its power being traditionally ascribed to the gods of Rome; also, in the Pauline period, the custom was growing of worshipping the emperor as a god. On the whole there was little need for the Romans to carry on religious persecution; they cheerfully comprehended local pagan religions within their system. The Jews, with their rigid faith in their own God were a special case; it was recognised that for a Jew to refuse homage to the Roman gods was not, as with anyone else, necessarily an expression of political disloyalty. Thus the Jews were allowed special exemptions from public worship; in return, they offered sacrifice for the emperor in the Jerusalem Temple. The first Christians counted as Jews and so they automatically benefited from the Jewish privileges. But the Pauline method of admitting members on baptism only, with no requirement to follow detailed Jewish practices, obviously caused strains. Mainstream Jews themselves could reasonably resent their privileges being claimed by people who were not proper Jews at all; the Roman authorities would be suspicious of fraud. It would be interesting to know, in this connection, the extent to which, if any, the God-fearers associated with synagogues were allowed Jewish exemptions; no evidence exists about it. In the general imbroglio, Paul suffered physical assault from both Jews and Romans; on a visit to Jerusalem he had to be rescued by Roman soldiers from a hostile Jewish crowd. Comparing himself with rival teachers, Paul wrote: 'I have been sent to prison more often, and whipped so many times more almost to death. Five times I had the thirty-nine lashes from the Jews; three times I have been beaten with sticks; once I was stoned.'[27] (It should be added that Paul in this passage apologises for the necessity of boasting about his own sufferings.)

However, as with nearly everything else in early Christianity, it is essential to grasp the Jewish background. Paul whether he liked it or not was inevitably talking politics in saying that the Christ was due to return in glory. The Jewish rebellion against Rome in A.D. 66 was based specifically upon belief in the Christ, who was seen by many as a wonder-working leader who would enable the Jews to defeat superior forces. Besieged in Jerusalem, the rebels hung on and on in the hourly expectation of a miracle that would save them; the failure of the miracle to happen then, and in the later rebellion of 132, fundamentally changed the character of Judaism. To any Roman, Paul's talk of the Christ automatically sounded like treason. Similarly, many Jews considered it dangerous: the rebels were only one faction in Judaism and very many Jews, both in Palestine and in the dispersion, regarded excitement about the Christ as damaging to their faith and community. The Jewish historian Josephus, for example, fought on the Roman side. By going on about the Christ, Paul, it could be held, was bringing Judaism into disrepute.

Paul did his best to make it plain that his doctrine of the Christ involved no political threat to Rome. If anything, he went on the side of extravagance in enjoining loyalty to the civil power. 'You must obey all the governing authorities. Since all government comes from God, the civil authorities were appointed by God, and so anyone who resists authority is rebelling against God's decision . . . all government officials are God's officers.'[28] The writings attributed to Peter are even more specific: 'For the sake of the Lord, accept the authority of every social institution: the emperor, as the supreme authority, and the governors commissioned by him . . . God wants you to be good citizens.'[29] Short of actually worshipping the emperor as divine, it would be difficult to take a higher view of Roman authority; such texts were to play a key part in seventeenth century English controversies over the powers of the Stuart monarchy. Presumably the matter was stressed in an attempt to differentiate the Christians from the Jewish rebels. To some extent it worked; persecution of the Christians by the Romans was sporadic rather than continuous and varied greatly in different times and different places. The Romans did not have 'thought police' systematically to root out cults they disliked. The Christians themselves never rose in revolt.

The first major Roman offensive against the Christians appears to have been in Rome itself under the Emperor Nero in A.D. 64. The occasion is interesting because it provides the earliest reference to Christianity by an outside writer, Tacitus. Writing about the event some forty years after it happened, Tacitus describes a fire that had devastated Rome and how Nero decided to blame the Christians for it. (Fire coming down from heaven was a thing the Christians talked much about.) 'The name was derived from Christ, who was executed under Tiberius the emperor and the procurator, Pontius Pilate,' wrote Tacitus. 'Suppressed for a moment, this execrable superstition broke out again not only in Judaea, where it began, but even in the city of Rome where all things base and shameful flow together and enjoy a vogue. Therefore, those first were taken who confessed, then on their testimony a vast multitude was convicted, not so much on the charge of arson as of hatred of the human race. A sport was made of their execution. Some, sewn in the skins of animals, were torn apart by dogs. Others were crucified or burned, and still others, as darkness drew on, were used as torches. Nero devoted his gardens to the spectacle, provided a circus, and himself, in the costume of a charioteer, rode around among the crowd, until compassion began to arise for the victims, who though deserving of the severest penalties were actually suffering not for the public good but to glut the cruelty of one man.' The tradition is that Peter died during this pogrom by being crucified upside down. Unfortunately Tacitus gives no indication of numbers; the term 'vast multitude' applied to executions might mean a few hundred. In mentioning the execution of Jesus under Pontius Pilate, Tacitus presumably was taking the Christians at their word rather than referring to actual Roman records; however, his easy acceptance of the fact seems to indicate that it was uncontroversial.

Paul, by tradition, escaped death in the Nero pogrom. He is supposed to have been executed at Rome by beheading (as befitted a Roman citizen) in about A.D. 67, that is during the Jewish revolt in Palestine. The exact circumstances are unknown but it is a reasonable guess that his propagation of

Jewish-Christian doctrines was enough at such a moment to count as treason.

Towards the end of his last letter, he writes his own obituary. He realises that the Christ is unlikely to come in his lifetime. 'As for me, my life is already being poured away as a libation, and the time has come for me to be gone. I have fought the good fight to the end; I have run the race to the finish; I have kept the faith; all there is to come now is the crown of righteousness reserved for me, which the Lord, the righteous judge will give me on that Day; and not only to me but to all those who have longed for his Appearing.'[30]

1 Acts 23:6
2 1 Cor 2:2
3 Acts 5:38–39
4 Acts 9:4–5
5 Gal 1:15–20
6 1 Cor 11:23
7 1 Cor 15:8
8 Mt 28:19
9 Gal 1:16
10 Col 4:6
11 Is 60:11
12 2 Pet 3:8–10
13 1 Thess 4:15–17
14 1 Cor 13:1–13
15 Rom 12:14–19
16 1 Cor 7:1–5; 8–9
17 Rom 10:9
18 2 Thess 1:8–9
19 1 Cor 7:31
20 1 Tim 2:5
21 1 Tim 5:23
22 1 Tim 3:1–16
23 1 Tim 3:8–12
24 1 Tim 5:17–20
25 1 Cor 11:21–22
26 1 Cor 11:28–34
27 2 Cor 11:23–25
28 Rom 13:1–2; 6
29 1 Pet 2:13–15
30 2 Tim 4:6–8

VIII

Who Wrote the New Testament?

Up until about A.D. 150 Christianity was an underground, semi-secret movement. Most of its history until then is a matter of the utmost obscurity. Since this is the period in which the New Testament cohered towards substantially its present form, the lack of information is historically a tragic one. There are many who would maintain that the New Testament and, in particular, the four gospels are the most important documents ever written. Actual wars have been fought over the meaning of New Testament texts. Unknown multitudes of people have had their lives influenced by them. To this day they are read aloud to congregations across the world. They have been translated into more than 1,000 languages. Their sales total something like ten million a year. In the law courts of fifty countries they are used in the routine oath of a witness. In Britain, every commissioner for oaths — that is a senior solicitor entitled to take written evidence to go before the courts — keeps a New Testament in his desk drawer; it is often tattered, not through having been read but only through having been held so often by witnesses: the law treats the volume as if it had some quasi-magical power to influence people to tell the truth. There is an association, the Gideons, which attempts to get the Bible or the New Testament, sometimes in multi-lingual form, on display in every hotel bedroom in the world. Issuing the New Testament is probably the most lucrative form of publishing there is for the people who are established in it. Britain has four times as many full-time clergymen as it has dentists and each cleric accounts the New Testament the principal written authority for his profession.

Yet who, exactly, wrote, revised and edited the various New Testament documents and exactly when and for exactly what motives remains a mystery. Over the past century enormous scholarship has been applied to the texts. Various methods of form criticism, source criticism and redaction criticism have distinguished different layers in them. Some more remains to be done in this direction. Computers may be of value in form criticism in establishing the styles of individual writers. Further work is needed on relating contemporaneous Jewish documents, including the Dead Sea scrolls, to the New Testament; the major deficiency of the older New Testament scholarship was that it took insufficient account of the Jewish background. At one extreme, some hold that a really rigorous philological examination of the gospels, using modern techniques, tends to show them as having been written in a secret code and that they were never intended to be taken at their face value: such a theory will require overwhelming proof before it commands acceptance. However, short of some such all-embracing explanation coming up, it is unlikely that scholarly research will do more than to modify or refine existing mainstream theories. The really big questions about the authorship of the gospels may remain for ever a mystery.

The point is that the early Christian groups which produced the New Testament were small, scattered, largely illiterate and secret or semi-secret. Guessing what is really unguessable, it can be conjectured that in the year A.D. 100 there were 100,000 Christians, as against about four million Jews and forty million inhabitants of the Roman Empire as a whole. Their proportionate strength was roughly equivalent to that of the Mormons in today's U.S.A.

Christianity was mainly or wholly an urban faith and communication between the groups in different cities, although it did go on, was unsystematic. There was no central, ruling

authority and probably there was a wide divergence in the
practices and even beliefs of different groups; it was to be a
further two centuries before it is possible, from a detached
viewpoint, to define what was orthodox 'catholic' Christianity
and what was 'heresy'. Every indication is that the bulk of
the members were of the lower classes, including slaves, and
that the level of literacy, sophistication and knowledge of the
world was low; Christians, generally, were far less intellectual than Jews. (Some of the Christian leaders, however,
must have been men of exceptional calibre.) The language of
the Christians, including those in Rome itself, was Greek, the
popular tongue of the Empire, not the Latin of the ruling
classes. Secrecy was used partly because of persecution and
partly because it was thought that the more sacred rites of
the faith ought to be private. To this day, the technical
division of the Roman Catholic mass is into the 'Mass of the
Catechumens', which consists of prayers and scripture read-
ings, and the 'Mass of the Faithful' in which the bread and
wine is consecrated. Although the whole thing is now public
and anyone may attend, the original idea was that pro-
spective converts should attend the first part, for purposes of
instruction, but should be barred from the second part until
they had been accepted into full membership. Most Christian
bodies still have restrictions on who may actually consume
the consecrated elements. The 'orthodox' churches of
eastern Europe and the Arab countries, which at the beginning of the twentieth century comprised one third of the
world Christian body, screen off their altars with curtains in
continuation of the custom of secrecy. Anyone who attends
service in the indigenous churches of the principal Christian
shrines associated directly with Jesus, that is in Jerusalem,
Bethlehem and Nazareth, finds that he is excluded by curtains from seeing the inner rites of the eucharist.

The secrecy of the aboriginal Christians led to their being
accused of wicked practices; it was the small change of anti-
Christian abuse to say that they held sex orgies and indulged

in cannibalism. Whether there was any truth at all in such charges is impossible to establish with final certainty but every probability is against them. Some have tried to detect such things as sorcery, drug-taking and fertility cults in early Christianity but the obstacle to such theories is that such things had certainly ceased to exist by A.D. 150, which is when documentary evidence begins to become plentiful. The only safe working assumption is that the Christianity of A.D. 150 was an evolution from that of A.D. 100 with no revolutionary break in the general tone of its customs. It is very easy to account for abusive allegations. People always think of orgies when they hear of groups meeting in secret; the more extravagant opponents of modern freemasonry allege sexual scandals. The cannibalism charge could easily have grown from a misunderstanding of the eucharist. Inspired prophets, speaking in 'tongues', could sound like sorcerers. Indeed to draw the boundary between religion and sorcery requires a sophistication which many of the critics of early Christianity would not have possessed.

The guiding principle in examining the New Testament is that it was the early Christian Church which produced the New Testament, not the New Testament which produced the early Christian Church. Thus to understand these documents, in historical terms, it is necessary to clasp such shreds of information about the thought of the early Church as are available, always keeping in mind that information is so sparse that it is safer to guess than to dogmatize. In the second century it produced masses of documents about the life of Jesus—the 'apocryphal gospels'—but these are mostly full of childish miracles and of little or no historical value; with no apparent difficulty the more cautious elements in the Church eventually got them excluded from the official New Testament.

It is a reasonable assumption that the death of the early leaders, notably Paul, caused no slackening in the impetus of Christian expansion. There must have been an enthusiastic second generation of leaders who kept things going in difficult circumstances. They had the particular problem that the Christ had failed to return in glory as had been promised. After fifty years of preaching that this event was imminent they might have been expected to begin to lose the confidence of their converts. However, it is a peculiarity of religious psychology that some people will go on believing apocalyptic promises long after they have been apparently unfulfilled. The prime modern example is Jehovah's Witnesses, who are conducting the most energetic propaganda across the world and still expanding despite the fact that their original prophesies about the imminent return of the Christ in our own day appear, on the face of it, to have been proved incorrect. In the same way, the failure of prophecies seems to have caused little serious embarrassment to the early Christians. They had a sense of personal communication with Jesus, to whom they prayed and whom they believed helped them; this was crucial in the development of the doctrine of Jesus's divinity.

One way of overcoming the apocalyptic problem was to focus attention away from the Christ and back to the personality of Jesus. To Paul, apparently, Jesus's teachings and biography were unimportant compared with the wonder of his return in glory. Now, however, a double process took place. On the one hand information was gathered about Jesus's human life. A lot of it, certainly, was based on the writer's view of what ought to have been his life, rather than what was his life, and many of the early Jesus biographies were excluded from the canon of the New Testament. On the other hand there was much thought of Jesus leading the Christians not in the flesh, as the returned Christ, but as a purely heavenly figure. Instead of Jesus's physical withdrawal being regarded as temporary, as Paul had regarded it, his being invisible and in heaven became the normal framework of the faith. His heavenly status, naturally, was exalted as high as possible and the doctrine grew up that he was identical

with God. On this, as on most early Christian matters,
it is fruitless to get polemical. Modern Christians, of the
orthodox kind, say that the development of the doctrine of
the divinity of Jesus was the logical result of prolonged
reflection upon the impact Jesus had made. A sceptical view
is that an invisible Jesus was so less an obviously dramatic
figure than the physical Christ returning to earth in glory
that it was necessary for propaganda reasons for the Church
to magnify his heavenly status. Neither explanation necessarily excludes the other. The early Christian leaders were
men who felt genuinely inspired and that they were the
bearers of a supremely important message — had they not
felt this, they would be incomprehensible. At the same time
they were successful propagandists and their priority was to
get converts rather than to observe the more meticulous rules
of historical writing. At any rate, by early in the second
century A.D. it had become the mainstream Christian doctrine that Jesus had been an incarnation of God in human
form. The idea that he was the Jewish Christ — that is a
miraculous leader operating physically in the world — was
beginning to fall into the background. The title 'Christ'
continued in use among Christians but with no exact meaning; today it is commonly used as if it were a surname. It
survives in its original sense among the ultra-orthodox Jews
in the Mea Shearim quarter of modern Jerusalem; they await
the Christ and regard the secular State of Israel as a
blasphemous anticipation of his coming.

The recognition of Jesus as God marked the complete
separation of Christianity from Judaism. There did subsist
for several centuries a tiny group of Jewish Christians who,
apparently, believed in a non-divine Jesus and continued to
observe Jewish practices but they are known only through the
writings of their opponents. The extent to which they were
the direct continuation of the original Disciples of Jesus in
Jerusalem is unknown and, in any event, they were of little
historical importance. The vast majority of both Jews and

Christians drew steadily further apart, a process which continued until the twentieth century and is now only just at the beginning of being reversed.

Sheer thought and theology had a lot to do with it.

It is a common Christian error to think that Jews who failed to accept Jesus were left as a stagnant rump, stuck in the first century, and that all new thought on the nature of God and on the relationship between God and man was Christian. In fact the Jews were at least as active as the Christians in developing their faith. Defeat at the hands of the Romans radically changed the nature of Judaism. The conservative party of the Sadducees disappeared because with the destruction of the Temple it no longer had an economic base. Similarly the Zealots, the militantly anti-Roman group, were discredited. Leadership fell to rabbis whose spiritual descent was from the old Pharisee party and they redefined Judaism as a primarily spiritual force and, in the Mishnah and the Talmud, produced the Jewish equivalent of the Christian New Testament. The doctrine of the Christ fell into the background. Ultimately, by the fifth century, Judaism had reached substantially its modern, normative form; it was a religion of great vitality which, uniquely, was to flourish on an entirely voluntary basis with no political support and sometimes subjected to persecution. Instead of the Temple, the home and the synagogue became its centre and this gave it flexibility and staying power. Largely through a desire to live at peace, it ceased to seek converts and became an almost entirely hereditary religion. By the fifth century, Judaism had changed nearly as much as Christianity had done. The first century Judaism of Hillel and Jesus is best reckoned as the common ancestor of modern Judaism and of modern Christianity; which line of descent is the more legitimate is a question capable of endless argument.

Exactly how or where the doctrine of the divinity of Jesus entered Christianity is unknown. There is no evidence of any particular teacher proclaiming it as a novelty and gaining converts to it. The best assumption must be that it grew up more or less spontaneously among second-generation Christians, of non-Jewish background, towards the end of the first century A.D. It is often held that such Christians, lacking in strict Jewish training but accustomed to the multiplicity of pagan gods, found the God-man a more comprehensible idea than that of the Jewish Christ. Every Roman emperor, on his death, was accounted a god. The more orthodox Christian view is that it simply took a period of mental digestion before the full implications of Jesus were understood but for this there is no evidence, either.

The first three gospels, those attributed to Matthew, Mark and Luke (to put them in their traditional order) do not affirm in any complete manner the divinity of Jesus but present him as the Christ. They grew out of oral traditions and, after they had been written down, continued to be amended by editors. It is impossible to date them precisely but it can be taken that they grew towards substantially their present form in the years A.D. 60–100. Who the authors were is unknown for certain. This is because of the very common Jewish-Christian custom of the time of a religious author seeking to get extra authority for his work by suppressing his own name and stating that it had been written by some famous person: this should not be accounted forgery or falsification in any modern sense—it was a recognised convention. Were it not for the existence of this custom, the tradition of Matthew, Mark and Luke being the authors could be taken solely at its face value, there being nothing inherently improbable in it. Matthew is held to have been a tax collector who was converted to Jesus and became one of the Twelve; the gospel in his name concentrates on attempting to prove that Jesus's life fulfilled Old Testament prophecies of the Christ. Mark is held to have been a companion of Peter and the short gospel in his name is said to enshrine Peter's own reminiscences. Luke is held to have been a medical doctor who worked with Paul.

Although on some points these three gospels are inconsistent, the striking thing about them is that they have passages of almost word for word similarity. Modern scholarship has sought to show how they copied from each other and probably, also, from other documents now lost. Passions have been particularly hot on whether Mark was the earliest to be written or whether, in fact, some form of Matthew really came first. The answers are unlikely ever to be known for certain and are likely to be complicated rather than simple.

In these gospels, Jesus is not yet fully deified but two crucial steps on the way towards this are taken.

The first is the dating of the crucifixion to coincide with the Jewish Seder festival, the moment of Jesus's death being that at which the paschal lambs were being slaughtered in the Temple. For reasons already discussed, this is inherently improbable and is approximately equivalent to a modern Christian execution taking place on Christmas Day. Paul in his letters makes no mention of it. However, all the gospels are in agreement upon it and so the possibility must be recognised that this strange timing did occur. The temptation, however, must be to reckon that Jesus dying at the same time as the paschal lambs was introduced for theological rather than historical reasons. To the audience for which the gospels were written, the coincidence of the two things would be a dramatic underpinning of the doctrine of Jesus's death being an atonement for sin. The modern mind, however, is more suspicious of coincidences. A later embellishment, taught at least until the nineteenth century, was that the crucifixion had taken place on the grave of Adam.

The second step towards deification is the unexpected doctrine of the virgin birth.

The Jews had a clear tradition of great men being born in quasi-miraculous circumstances. The ordinary pattern was for the parents of such a personality to be past the ordinary age of child-bearing; this is stated to have happened with Isaac and, also, in the Jesus period, with John the Baptist.

Nowhere, however, in the Jewish tradition is there any case of a great man being born of a virgin without a human father. Pagan religions are full of stories of the gods having intercourse with human women to produce wonderful children, such as Romulus, founder of Rome, and the temptation is to suppose that the doctrine of the virgin birth was introduced into Christianity under pagan rather than Jewish auspices. However, there is no positive evidence of how or why it came in.

One explanation could be that it came in, simply, by mistake. In the book of Isaiah occurs the statement: 'the young woman is with child and will soon give birth to a son'.* In the Greek version, the Septuagint, used by the early Christians, this is mistranslated so that 'young woman' becomes 'virgin'. In its context, the prophecy has nothing to do with the coming of the Christ but such was the Jewish-Christian use of the scriptures at that time that there is nothing surprising in it being pressed into service in connection with Jesus. Could a staggering theology have been erected upon an error of translation by scholars in Alexandria? There is no doubt that the Septuagint version is an error. However it is arguable that the text is likely to have been brought into use as a result rather than the cause of the virgin birth doctrine.

But what, exactly, did the Jews of the time mean by the word virgin? There is some indication from roughly contemporary rabbinical sources that 'virgin' to a first century Jew need not have the ordinary connotation of a woman who had never experienced sexual intercourse. To at least some rabbis, a virgin was a girl who had not yet menstruated. (The subject of menstruation was an important one in Jewish teachings on sex and purity.) Given the custom of early marriage, it was possible for some girls to experience

* Since generally the scriptural quotations in this book are in the English of the Jerusalem Bible, it should be stated that the Jerusalem Bible uses 'maiden', not 'young woman' in the Isaiah passage. When the same passage is quoted in Matthew, the Jerusalem Bible uses legitimately 'virgin'.

intercourse before they had reached puberty and imaginable that in some cases they conceived a child at their first ovulation and thus bore it while they were still, technically, in a state of virginity. Another possibility, of a similar kind, springs from involved rabbinical rulings on the rupturing of the hymen. The only technical proof permitted was the shedding of blood. If a girl failed to shed blood on her wedding night, the husband had some right to repudiate her as 'damaged goods'. To be 'born of a virgin' in some such technical sense might be remarkable enough for it to be long remembered of the baby but it would carry no miraculous connotation. However, when the statement 'his mother was a virgin' was repeated to people ignorant of Jewish teaching they would naturally tend to take it as a miracle in line with the miracles of the pagan deities. While it would be unwise to accept this as a definitive explanation of the 'virgin birth' it does offer an interesting line of speculation. It may be observed, incidentally, that traditions that Jesus's mother was seduced by a Roman soldier or some other man and deceived her fiancé into believing her pregnancy was the work of God are late and spring from professed anti-Christians.

There are, really, two stories of the virgin birth, given at the beginnings of the gospels of Matthew and Luke. (The other gospels do not mention it.) The two stories are inconsistent and can safely be taken to belong to different sources.

The Matthew birth story is the earlier and may, in its original form, have contained no virginity at all. It centres around the 'carpenter' Joseph, who lived in Bethlehem. It starts off with Joseph's genealogy showing him to be a descendant of Abraham and David. The arrangement is ritualistic so that it falls into three groups of fourteen generations each and the natural ending would be to show Joseph as the father of Jesus; one old manuscript actually has this. But the accepted text has a sharp break in style so that it ends: 'and Jacob was the father of Joseph the husband of

Mary; of her was born Jesus who is called Christ.'[1] Does this break in style mark the hand of an editor adjusting an original text to bring it into line doctrinally? Certainly it is difficult to see why the genealogy is given if Joseph were not Jesus's father. (Conjectures that Mary and Joseph were cousins and so shared the same genealogy have no historical warrant.)

The story goes on to Joseph getting betrothed to Mary; but he found she was pregnant and decided, informally, not to go on with the marriage. Then an angel appeared to him in a dream and told him that the child had been conceived by the Holy Spirit. Joseph accepted this, took Mary into his home and the boy, Jesus, was born. (There is no mention of a stable and the inescapable implication is that the birth took place at home in the ordinary way.)

Then follows a passage in which the early infancy of Jesus is presented as being similar to that of the Jewish hero Moses. According to the Old Testament, Moses was born at a time when the Egyptians were slaughtering Israelite male babies; his mother hid him away and this led to his being preserved. Supplementary Jewish traditions, which were widely current in the first century, had both the Egyptian Pharoah and the parents being warned in dreams of the baby's future greatness, this being the cause of the wholesale slaughter. Similarly the Matthew version of Jesus's infancy has the Judaean King Herod ordering a mass killing at Bethlehem of male babies because he has been told that one of them was 'king of the Jews'. (There is no evidence, beyond the Matthew text, that so startling an event as 'the slaughter of the innocents' ever took place; it thus looks infinitely more probable that it was made up for reason of the Moses parallel than that it really happened.) Joseph is warned in a dream of Herod's intentions and immediately takes the wife and baby into hiding in Egypt. Later, as a result of another dream of Joseph's, the family settles in Nazareth. As part of the mechanism of the story, a group of 'wise men' visited Jesus's cradle, directed to it by a star. The best definition of them is that they were supposed to be non-Jewish astrologers acknowledging the baby's greatness as the Christ. The tradition that they were kings and that there were three of them is not in the gospel and sprung up later on the basis of Old Testament prophecies. The star, however, was a normal messianic emblem; Simon bar-Cochba, who during the Jewish revolt of A.D. 132 was hailed as the Christ, had the star minted on the coins he issued.

The Luke account is radically different from the Matthew one and is later. The virgin birth is integral to it rather than a possible later addition as in Matthew. It has no wise men, no flight to Egypt and no slaughter of babies by Herod. Joseph's genealogy is given but is completely different from the Matthew one, even his father's name being different. The central figure in Luke, however, is not Joseph but Mary; instead of the course of events being determined by Joseph's dreams it is determined by angels appearing to Mary while she is awake. Mary, naturally, is in an exalted condition and is described as speaking words of nobility upon which much subsequent theology has been erected. Her main speech, still frequently used in Christian services as the 'Magnificat', seems to be an early Christian hymn which the gospel writer put into her mouth. In the breadth and universality of its ideas it gives a clue to the atmosphere in which the gospel was written and accepted; as with so much else in early Christianity, it is useless to concentrate on the quaint side without taking into account the permanent significance of part of the emotions of the men who made it. The 'Magnificat' proclaims the glory of humility and poverty: it must be taken as an authentic voice of the early Christian church.

'My soul proclaims the greatness of the Lord
and my spirit exults in God my saviour;
because he has looked upon his lowly handmaid.
Yes, from this day forward all generations will call me
   blessed,

for the Almighty has done great things for me.
Holy is his name,
and his mercy reaches from age to age for those who fear
  him.
He has shown the power of his arm,
he has routed the proud of heart.
He has pulled down princes from their thrones and exalted
  the lowly.
The hungry he has filled with good things, the rich sent
  empty away . . .'[2]

This at least approaches the grandeur of the psalms of
mainstream Judaism and has some flavour of socialism to it.
It was the kind of thing the early Christians recited when
they were being executed for their faith.

Joseph's reaction to Mary's miraculous pregnancy is not
recorded in Luke, save that he does stick by her. Instead of
them being residents of Bethlehem, as in Matthew, they
belong to Nazareth. The two places are about eighty miles
apart, about a three days' journey, and were of an entirely
different character. Nazareth (assuming that the biblical
town was the same place as the modern one) was an important centre in the rich, cosmopolitan Galilee province; it had
become Jewish only through the recent conquests of the
Hasmoneans and had no significance in Jewish religious
tradition. Bethlehem, just south of Jerusalem, belonged to the
Jewish heartland of Judaea; it was the traditional birthplace
of King David and it had been prophesied that the Christ
would be born there too. The writer of Luke knew, presumably, that Joseph and Mary belonged to Nazareth but it
was essential to fulfil the prophecy that Jesus was born in
Bethlehem. (Also he may have known the Matthew tradition
about the birth being in Bethlehem.) Accordingly he adopts
the strange device of Joseph and Mary travelling to Bethlehem for an imperial census which required every man to
register 'in his own town'. Joseph, as a descendant of David,

had to register in Bethlehem. It is surprising that Luke could
get away with this—neither the Romans nor anyone else ever
conducted a census in such a chaotic manner: conceivably
there was some supplementary information now lost and
unguessable at. At Bethlehem Mary gives birth to Jesus and,
because there is no room at the inn, puts him into a feeding
manger for livestock. (The presumption has always been that
the birth took place in a stable, although this is not stated.)
Angels call shepherds from the fields to go and look at the
baby. Instead of fleeing to Egypt, Joseph and Mary call at
Jerusalem to present the baby as their first-born at the
Temple and then go home to Nazareth. The Temple priest is
represented as speaking words which were another very early
Christian hymn:

> 'Now, Master, you can let your servant go in peace,
> just as you promised;
> because my eyes have seen the salvation
> which you have prepared for all the nations to see,
> a light to enlighten the pagans
> and the glory of your people Israel.'[3]

After the Matthew and Luke birth stories had reached
their definitive form, Christian tradition continued to
develop them. Despite the disparities between them, they
were for popular purposes merged into a single account; the
main framework used was that of Luke, with the star, wise
men and flight to Egypt inserted from Matthew. The 'stable'
scene was amplified by the introduction of an ox and an ass,
presumably on the basis of the Isaiah prophecy: 'the ox
knows its owner and the ass its master's crib, Israel knows
nothing, my people understand nothing.'[4] Eventually it came
to be held by some that the ox and the ass were temporarily
given the power of speech. The wise men were promoted to
the rank of kings, the basis being prophecies in Isaiah—'The
nations come to your light and kings to your dawning bright-
ness'[5]—and in Psalm 72—'The kings of Sheba and Seba will

offer gifts; all kings will do him homage.'[6] Joseph came to be represented as an elderly widower: elderly to account for the belief that Mary remained a lifelong virgin and a widower to enable him to have had children by a previous wife who were the 'brothers' of Jesus mentioned in the gospels. Words spoken to Mary in Luke—'Rejoice, so highly favoured!'[7] and 'Of all women you are the most blessed'[8]—are the scriptural foundations for the Roman Catholic doctrines that Mary lacked original sin and on her death was taken physically into heaven, defined as dogma in the nineteenth and twentieth centuries respectively.

The process at every stage shows how prophecies were used to establish facts and then facts, so established, were used to erect further facts. For purposes of scientific history such a procedure is useless. However, the writers of Matthew and Luke and the later amplifiers of the birth story were inspired not by historical but by doctrinal and ritualistic motives. What counted was to place the birth of Jesus in what looked like a suitable setting. The results cannot be counted as biographical in the way that the reports of the sayings of Jesus can, as a working hypothesis, safely be regarded as on the whole historically credible.

The crowning stone of the edifice of Christian doctrine was that Jesus was actually divine. This is almost absent from the first three gospels but it begins to appear in the very different fourth gospel, that of John. Because of its richness in doctrine, many Christians prefer John's late gospel for devotional reading to the rather sparse and dry accounts in the first three gospels. The John given as the author has traditionally been held to be the same John who was called by Jesus to be one of the Twelve and to whose care Jesus handed his mother Mary: John is supposed to have written it while living on the island of Patmos in extreme old age, in about A.D. 100. Bishop Polycarp of Smyrna, an undoubtedly historical figure who was martyred in A.D. 150, said that as a youth he had actually met John, who was an attractive old man. Because of his vast age, John had to be carried to church on Sundays and he repeated over and again the same brief sermon: 'Little children, love one another.' The gospel contains two principal ingredients which are inconsistent with each other and even clash. The first is straightforward biographical information about Jesus which, historically, forms a useful supplement to that given in the first three gospels. The second ingredient is lashings of highly theological statements put into the mouth of Jesus as set discourses, covering such subjects as baptism, the eucharist, the conflict between darkness and light, the atonement, the resurrection and the Holy Spirit. Quite possibly the gospel is the work of two different authors, the one setting out authentic, first-hand recollections of Jesus and the other doing the elaborate theology.

In John, the doctrine of the Christ and his imminent return, is beginning to fall into the background. The gospel opens with what appears to be a hymn in which Jesus is presented as the eternal 'Word'. (The idea that God had created such a Word is also found in the Jewish-Greek Philo of Alexandria.) It is worth quoting as yet another example of the kind of thing the earliest Christians were reciting at their meetings:

> 'In the beginning was the Word:
> the Word was with God
> and the Word was God.
> He was with God in the beginning.
> Through him all things came to be,
> not one thing had its being but through him . . .
> . . . The Word was made flesh,
> he lived among us,
> and we saw his glory,
> that glory that is his as the only Son of the Father . . .'[9]

This, immediately, begins to convert Jesus from Son of

God, that is a Jewish holy man, into the infinitely greater 'God the Son'. Later, the gospel has Jesus using the forbidden name of God, 'I Am', and stating: 'To have seen me is to have seen the Father . . . I am in the Father and the Father is in me.'[10]

John is particularly interesting on the eucharist, the ceremonial meal of the Christians. He has Jesus announcing the highest doctrine on it: 'I tell you most solemnly, if you do not eat the flesh of the Son of Man and drink his blood, you will not have life in you. Anyone who does eat my flesh and drink my blood has eternal life.'[11] Yet the account of the last supper, although lengthy and highly theological, contains no mention of the eucharist being instituted. This would seem to indicate the possibility that the Christian meal originated from the general background of Jewish ceremonial meals rather than from any startling innovation by Jesus: John is silent on how bread and wine become the flesh and blood of Jesus which it is obligatory to eat and drink.

Despite the unJewish trend towards making Jesus divine, John's gospel draws generously from Jewish sources. The idea of the Word belongs to the philosophy of Philo. There is also a stress upon the struggle between light and darkness and between God and Satan which in phraseology is close to that found in the scrolls of the Qumran sect. 'While you still have the light, believe in the light and you will become sons of light', Jesus is quoted as saying. 'I, the light, have come into the world.'[12] The Qumran sect often described its members as 'the sons of light'.

John's gospel finds it necessary to be emphatic on the point that Jesus had really lived as a human being. Already in A.D. 100 when, if the conventional chronology is accepted, Jesus had been dead for only seventy years, there was a school of thought, the Docetists, which maintained that he had not been a man but only a phantom. In the early centuries of Christianity this kind of idea kept bobbing up and down in various heretical groups. It reflects the essentially

elusive nature of Jesus's personality and the historical possibility that it was in fact accurate cannot be totally neglected,
although it is most improbable. ('Accurate' in the sense either
that Jesus was a group-hallucination or else a figure deliberately invented for Jewish mystical purposes of a nature
which is not clear.) The writer of John, however, is doggedly
persistent about the full humanity of Jesus. He gives the
homely miracle of the wedding feast at which Jesus turned
water into wine. He stresses 'we saw him'[13] and 'this is the
evidence of one who saw it—trustworthy evidence'.[14]

The warmth of John's gospel demonstrates better than
anything else in the New Testament the power of Christian
teaching; it is because these difficult documents correspond
with human wants and emotions that Christianity grew to its
present size. Using for a moment the King James I
Authorised Version of the Bible as that most familiar to
English speakers, it is worth selecting some quotations from
John which have moved many people. 'If any man thirst, let
him come unto me and drink.'[15] 'I am the light of the world;
he that followeth me shall not walk in darkness, but shall have
the light of life.'[16] 'I am the good shepherd: the good shepherd
giveth his life for the sheep.'[17] 'Peace I leave with you, my
peace I give unto you. Let not your heart be troubled,
neither let it be afraid.'[18] 'Ye are clean through the word
which I have spoken unto you.'[19] 'I am the vine, ye are the
branches: He that abideth in me, and I in him, the same
bringeth forth much fruit: for without me you can do
nothing.'[20] Such words have high literary quality and it is
easy to conclude that they bear a stamp of authority. One of
the most intriguing questions in the world must be the extent
to which they reflect the real Jesus of Nazareth as opposed to
the imagination of an eager theologian writing seventy years
later. But at any rate in John there now exists the rounded
image of Jesus as has been propagated in mainstream
Christianity ever since.

And the community which produced this doctrine?

Somewhere between the years A.D. 111 and 113, the younger Pliny, imperial Legate in Bithynia, northern Turkey, wrote a letter to the Emperor Trajan containing the earliest worthwhile independent evidence of the nature of the Christians. Bithynia was a troublesome area and Pliny had been given a special commission from the Emperor to quieten it down; he corresponded with the Emperor in detail on the problems he faced. One of his troubles, apparently, was a wide growth of Christianity which he did his best to check by capital punishment; he questioned the Christians about their behaviour and was told:

'What they were guilty of amounted to no more than this, that it was their habit on a fixed day to assemble before daylight and sing by turns [presumably antiphonally] a hymn to Christ as a god; and that they bound themselves by an oath, not for any crime but not to commit theft or robbery or adultery, not to break their word, and not to deny a deposit when demanded. After this was done, their custom was to depart and meet together again to take food but ordinary and harmless food: and even this they said they had given up doing after the issue of my edict by which, in accordance with your demands, I had forbidden the existence of clubs.'

[1] Mt 1:16	[8] Lk 1:42	[15] Jn 7:37
[2] Lk 1:46–53	[9] Jn 1:1–3; 14	[16] Jn 8:12
[3] Lk 2:29–32	[10] Jn 14:9; 11	[17] Jn 10:11
[4] Is 1:3	[11] Jn 6:53–54	[18] Jn 14:27
[5] Is 60:3	[12] Jn 12:46	[19] Jn 15:3
[6] Ps 72:10–11	[13] Jn 1:14	[20] Jn 15:5
[7] Lk 1:28	[14] Jn 19:35	

IX

Rivals and Heretics

IN the A.D. 90s there lived in Rome an enthusiastic Christian called Clement. He was either head of the Church in the city of Rome or else a prominent member of it; in retrospect he has been hailed as the fourth 'Pope' and his name appears in the canon of the Roman Catholic mass together with those of his predecessors Linus and Anacletus. (On this computation, the first 'Pope' was the apostle Peter.) Nothing is known of Linus or Anacletus, but Clement is a thoroughly historical personality whose memory lingered long and around whom many legends grew up. The crucial thing about him, from the historical point of view, is that one letter, of 10,000 words, survives from his pen. It is the earliest non-biblical Christian document that exists and so gives invaluable evidence of the nature of Christianity in the second generation. Clement refers to Peter and Paul as the founders of the Roman Church and, although he does not specifically say so, can reasonably be taken to have known them personally. In the early centuries of Christianity his letter was read at church services and was accounted by some to be a part of the Christian scriptures. However, it failed to get into the canon of the New Testament, as finally fixed in the fifth century, and for 1,000 years it passed into virtual oblivion. Not until 1875 was it first published in full in English. One reason for its disappearance in the west was that Clement wrote in Greek; for the first two centuries of its existence, Greek was the language of the Roman Church but for 1,000 years—roughly from A.D. 500 to 1,500—knowledge of Greek

was almost totally lost to western scholarship. In the east the
letter was preserved in manuscript, notably in Alexandria,
but does not seem to have attracted much attention until the
seventeenth century.

One line of tradition puts Clement socially very high
indeed and identifies him with Titus Flavius Clemens, cousin
of the reigning emperor Domitian. This Flavius Clemens
certainly existed. He served as consul in 95 and Domitian
adopted his two young sons as his heirs. The following year,
however, he fell into disfavour and Domitian executed him
on a charge of 'atheism' — that is of failing to perform pagan
religious duties. Such an identification is a romantic one and
indicates the fascinating possibility that Christianity came
near to being the official religion of the Roman Empire at a
very early stage. Unfortunately, the identification is almost
certainly wrong. The atheism charge against Flavius
Clemens is more likely to have been trumped up by a
capricious and cruel emperor than to indicate adherence to
Christianity; if it had any justification at all, it is more likely
to indicate that Flavius Clemens had some connection with
the Jews than with the Christians, the Jews being much more
prominent than the Christians. Every sign is that the early
Roman Christians were of low social status; there was no
more likelihood of their converting a member of the imperial
family than of a modern West Indian revivalist group, meeting in a private house in an immigrant quarter of London,
securing the adherence of the Duke of Kent. Apart from such
general considerations, Clement's letter was written by a man
soaked in Jewish scriptures and prophecies and so is unlikely
to have been the work of a gentile convert. The most likely
explanation of Clement is that he was a Greek-speaking
Jew. Perhaps he was a freedman who had originally been
taken to Rome as a slave after fighting in the Jewish rebellion of A.D. 66; the Christ had failed to come to aid the
Jews in that rebellion and so he turned to the type of Christ
preached by the Christians. At any rate, such an explanation

is more credible than that he was a Roman aristocrat.

Clement's letter, which in some retrospective sense can be called the first papal encyclical, shows that he considered Christianity to be the true form of Judaism rather than a separate religion. All his arguments are Jewish and, apart from Jesus, Peter and Paul, the only authorities he quotes are the Jewish patriarchs and prophets. He is deeply interested in the rites of the Jerusalem Temple, which had been destroyed only thirty years earlier. All this is a useful sidelight on the nature of the audience he wanted to influence and impress; anybody not thoroughly acquainted with Jewish teaching would find the letter incomprehensible. Perhaps Christianity in A.D. 100 was still a great deal more Jewish than many historians have recognised. Clement makes no specific statement of the divinity of Jesus but uses such forms as: 'The sceptre of the majesty of God, our Lord Jesus Christ, came not in show of pride and arrogance, though he could have done so, but with humility.' His quotations of Jesus's words indicate that he was familiar with at least some of the material of the first three gospels but he adds no biographical information of his own—his interest was in the mystical, resurrected Jesus rather than the real teacher. He mentions no virgin birth. He taught that Jesus's execution had been an atonement for the sins of mankind but urged, also, that men must do good deeds and not just rely on faith—'Let the rich man distribute to the necessity of the poor; and let the poor bless God that he has given unto him by whom their want may be supplied.'

The letter is addressed to the Church at Corinth in southern Greece, an important Christian centre where Paul had preached. Apparently the Corinthian Church had fallen into disorder or schism with some members trying to depose the leaders. Clement calls for peace. 'Wherefore are there strifes and angers and schisms and wars among us? Have we not all one God and one Christ? Is not the Spirit of grace poured out among us all? Have we not one calling in Christ? Why then do we rend and tear to pieces, and raise seditions against our own body? And are we come to such a height of madness as to forget that we were "members one of another"?' More specifically he demands obedience to the ecclesiastical authorities, likening the Christian organisation to that of the Jerusalem Temple. 'The chief priest has his proper services; and to the priests their proper place is appointed; and to the levites appertain their proper ministers; and the layman is confined within the bounds of what is commanded to laymen.' In the earliest statement of the doctrine of the 'apostolic succession', Clement says Christian ministers derive their authority from the apostles.

To what extent, in writing such a letter, was Clement behaving as a Pope?

This is a question over which Roman Catholic and Protestant scholars have squabbled endlessly and there is no clear answer. The letter is unlike modern papal documents in that it seeks to persuade rather than command; Clement does not claim jurisdiction over the Corinthian church. Moreover, the letter is written in the name of the whole Roman Church, not of Clement personally; he does not claim to be the personal successor to Peter. On the other hand, the letter shows that the Roman Church did feel it its business to offer strong advice to another Church that was in trouble; quite possibly it had been appealed to by one or other party in the Corinthian controversy. It is a fair assumption that because of its location in the huge capital city of the empire, its relatively large size and its past association with Peter and Paul, the Roman Church before A.D. 100 was already beginning to claim some special seniority. The process would have been speeded up by the virtual smashing of the original 'Jerusalem Church' in the Jewish revolts of 66 and 132. The actual word 'pope' is a corruption of the Greek word meaning 'father' and has no particular significance. The bishops of Alexandria called themselves 'popes' long before the bishops of Rome did and the title is still in use today in some of the eastern Churches as the designation of an ordinary parish priest. On one view it can be held that Clement's letter was the first visible step towards the doctrine defined 1,775 years later that the Bishop of Rome, when teaching formally, was infallible. Clement himself would probably have been surprised at such an idea and the best interpretation of his views must be the moderate one; extreme interpretations, either Roman Catholic or Protestant, are likely to be wrong.

'Strifes and angers and schisms and wars' wrote Clement and this was indeed a characteristic of early Christianity. Any idea that the Christians were a monolithic force steadily conquering the world with a set of agreed doctrines is utterly incorrect. They were a chaotic lot. Their remarkable doctrines of the Christ and of God having turned himself into a man inevitably caused excitement and far-reaching speculation. Even in the Pauline letters it is easy to detect how Christians tended to split into different factions, and this practice continued. It was encouraged by the high degree of independence of each other of the Churches scattered in different cities. Even such an apparently straightforward matter as the correct date on which to celebrate Easter caused centuries of controversy, some of it abusive; to this day Christians celebrate Easter on different dates. The growth of mainstream Catholic Christianity was a tortuous affair with many points at which a slight shift in balance would have produced a radically different end-product. There were varying traditions being handed down; for example the second century Basilides, who denied the resurrection of the body, claimed that he was following doctrine left by the apostles Peter and Matthias. It is only in retrospect that what was 'orthodoxy' and what was 'heresy' can be defined historically. Not until the Emperor of Rome had been converted and presided at the Council of Nicea in 325 did the Church reach some basis of unity, and even subsequently schisms continued to occur. In Great Britain today there are about ten major Christian denominations* plus several dozen minor or local ones. Although most of the churches still do not recognise each others' orders and do not permit inter-communion, the present generation has seen some growth in friendship and co-operation between them. The so-called 'ecumenical movement', which hopes for an eventual union of the Christian bodies, holds that the disunity is somehow unnatural. Actually the historical basis for such a belief is far from clear; schism has been as much a characteristic of Christianity as unity. Some of the more radical Christian thinkers want not so much unity as the dismantling of all the ecclesiastical structures. 'God forbid that the present churches should unite to form one, vast unified organisation', writes Mr. Charles Davis, the formerly Roman Catholic theologian who left his Church to become a sort of free-lance Christian.

Of the early Christian heresies, easily the most fascinating is that of Docetism, which claimed that Jesus of Nazareth had never existed as a man at all but only as a spirit. It certainly appeared very early, by about A.D. 100, and the gospel of John appears in part to have been written in an attempt to discredit it. Unfortunately, as with most of the early heresies, Docetism is known only through the writings of its opponents and so it is impossible to be too precise about it. The crucial question is whether it represented some genuine tradition which had been handed down or whether it was a mere intellectual speculation. It is remarkable that it was capable of being preached at a time when there were people still living who, according to the orthodox view, had actually met Jesus the man. If there were any shred of genuine tradition in it, the story of Jesus would become in some ways much

---

* Without counting separately such allied groups as the Church of England and the Scottish Episcopal Church, a list of ten can be formulated as follows: Church of England, Church of Scotland, Roman Catholics, Methodists, Baptists, Congregationalists, Pentecostalists, Welsh Calvinistic-Methodists, Free Church of Scotland, Christian Scientists. The powerful Salvation Army, which does not account itself a self-contained Church, could for practical purposes, be counted as an eleventh.

easier to understand. If he were only a spirit who inspired a group of people, the paucity of biographical information about him would be immediately explicable. Did the earliest Christians get their doctrine in visions in the same way that Paul of Tarsus did? However, short of some new discovery from such a source as the Dead Sea scrolls, the assumption must be that the orthodox tradition of Jesus living and teaching as a human being is, at least in outline, the more reliable; to suppose otherwise is to set an enormous puzzle over such personalities as Clement of Rome. The best explanation of Docetism is that it believed so deeply that the flesh and the world were evil that it was impossible for Jesus to be a part of them.

In one form and another Docetism bobbed up and down for at least three centuries; it was a basic raw material which could be used in many different forms of religious system.

The chief opponent of Docetism was Ignatius of Antioch, Syria, who, like Clement of Rome, looms out of the historical mist as one of the handful of known personalities in early Christianity. There are contradictory traditions about him but it is agreed that he was Bishop of Antioch in the early years of the second century and that he was the leading figure in the whole Christianity of the east. In about 115 he was arrested and taken to Rome and thrown to the lions in the arena. His journey to Rome had something of the air of a triumphal progress; he seems to have been loosely guarded and Christians thronged to see him and hear him preach in every city through which he passed. During the journey he wrote a number of letters of which at least seven survive. He was positively rejoicing in the prospect of martyrdom and urged the Roman Church not to do anything that would get him reprieved. When the lions had finished with him his friends picked up his remains, a few chawed bones, and took them back for burial at Antioch. Ignatius obviously regarded Docetism as a force both dangerous and virile. Writing of its adherents, Ignatius states: 'Some there are who carry about the name of Christ in deceitfulness, but do things unworthy of God; whom ye must flee, as ye would do so many wild beasts; for they are ravening dogs, who bite secretly — against whom ye must guard yourselves, as men hardly to be cured.'

He sets out fully the developed doctrine of the divine Jesus being born of a virgin and living as a man. '. . . Our God Jesus Christ was, according to the dispensation of God, conceived in the womb of Mary, of the seed of David, by the Holy Ghost; he was born and baptised . . . Now the virginity of Mary, and he who was born of her, were kept in secret from the prince of this world [Satan]; as was the death of our Lord: three of the mysteries the most spoken of throughout the world, yet done in secret by God. How then was our Saviour manifested to the world? A star shone in heaven beyond all other stars, and its light was inexpressible, and its novelty struck terror in men's minds . . . Hence all the power of magic became dissolved; and every bond of wickedness was destroyed; men's ignorance was taken away, and the old kingdom abolished; God himself appearing in the form of a man, for the renewal of eternal life.'

There is a romantic, unhistorical note in Ignatius, smacking of eastern mystery religions. With his stars and wonders he makes the squarely Jewish Clement of Rome look dull. His is the earliest unequivocal statement of the divinity of Jesus which is extant. He sounds as if he had never been Jewish at all — his letters show relatively little interest in the Old Testament and Jewish tradition — and, next to his dislike of Docetists ranked his dislike of Judaising tendencies in Christianity. It would be interesting to know to what extent, if any, his teachings were a novelty to the Roman Christians. However, he and Clement share an unshakeable and common characteristic; continually they stress the necessity for order and authority in the Church. The key person for both of them is the overseer, or bishop, who, they say, has been appointed by the apostles and stands for Jesus himself.

A bishop in their time was substantially different from a

modern bishop. There was no such territorial unit as the diocese — that came in only after Christianity had become the official religion of the state — and the unit was the local Church, the gathering of Christian believers. Doubtless in some cases, notably the strong Church of Rome, there were subordinate or branch Churches, but the regular rule was that Christian worship was incomplete without the bishop in person presiding over it. In some other cases it can be deduced that a local Church was ruled by a group of bishops rather than by a single one. As the second century proceeded the rule steadily became clearer of one Church, one bishop. ('Church' still meant a community of believers meeting, usually in private houses; it did not mean a building.) Subordinate to the bishops was an order of deacons who assisted at worship and, to some extent, looked after charitable and business activities. In a middle status, for long undefined, was a group of ministers who shared some but not all the authority of the bishop. They were called elders or presbyters, terms which were both originally Jewish, and priests, which was a universal word for religious officials. A bishop was elected by his Church but his appointment, it seems, had to be endorsed by neighbouring bishops. The laying on of hands was the normal means of conveying authority. Some Churches because of size or association with apostles claimed special rights of leadership, notably Rome and Antioch. It is useless for modern Christians to look back to this period for endorsement or otherwise of episcopal ecclesiastical government as it is now understood. Non-episcopalians can legitimately claim that a second century bishop was the equivalent of a parish priest and not the ruler of a large number of Churches. Episcopalians can point to the early development of a bishop's status towards something uniquely privileged; a second century bishop claimed and was allowed personal authority on a scale far beyond that of a modern minister of a non-episcopal Church. As with the papacy, and so much else in Christianity, it is historically impossible to seek models in the early Church for the present conduct of affairs. The delusion that it was possible to do so was the tragedy of the Protestant reformation in the sixteenth century; the reformers lacked historical information.

Government by bishops combined authority with flexibility and was a most effective instrument. It can safely be asserted that this system was in large measure responsible for the continuing advance of Christianity against persecution and against rival forms of faith. Almost none of the rival forms of religion had anything so effective — they depended either upon a single leader or had no real organisation at all. It can be taken for granted that many of the early Christian bishops must have been men of unusual ability and character. Most of them, during the second century, were probably of low social class and slight education, were dirty in their clothing and habits (until modern times there seems to have been a curious antipathy between Christianity and washing) and knew little of the world but, despite all this, they gave leadership and displayed courage. Then the magnifying of the office rather than the man meant that if a bishop were arrested and thrown to the lions a successor could be immediately chosen with precisely the same authority.

The importance of bishops can be seen, indirectly, in the heresy of Marcionism which grew up in the middle of the second century. Marcion was a rich shipowner who gave money to the Church of Rome but then branched out on his own with a new set of doctrines. (In excommunicating him, the Church of Rome gave him his money back.) Marcion eradicated the Old Testament and much of the New Testament from the Christian scriptures, said that Jesus had been a phantom, not a real man, and claimed that the God of the Jews was an inferior being to the higher God of the Christians revealed in Jesus. Very rapidly, Marcion built up a considerable organisation which, in some places, exceeded in strength the orthodox Christian Church. Perhaps his wealth was of some assistance in this but it is notable that he also copied exactly the Christian framework of bishops, priests and deacons; the result was that Marcionism, with its good organisation, was longer-lived than most other heretical groups. It lasted nearly two centuries. On occasion the orthodox and the Marcionites went to the lions together, ignoring each other's existence. Had the Marcionites won, the separation between Judaism and Christianity would have been taken to a logical conclusion instead of to the present ambivalent situation of the Christians still using Jewish scriptures but repudiating some of their meaning. (The obvious meaning, that is, not necessarily the special forms of interpretation put on them by classical Christian commentators.)

Much of the theoretical background to Marcionism and other heresies was provided by a strong system of religious thought called Gnosticism. Despite recent scholarly work on the subject, Gnosticism is not yet fully understood. It was an all-pervading system which influenced not only the heretical Christians but also many other religious groups, including the mainstream Christians and even Judaism. It appears to have sprung up in Babylon as a derivation of Zoroaster's Parsee religion and to have been elaborated in Egypt. There were many different forms of it but it was based, substantially, on the idea of special and secret 'knowledge' of the workings of the universe. It had a close association with astrology. The 'wise men' portrayed in Matthew's gospel as visiting the cradle of Jesus may well have some Gnostic or astrological significance. The leading idea seems to have been that the world and all physical objects had been created by a junior God, above whom stood a senior God who had created spirits. Thus men's bodies were controlled by the junior God but, through their souls, they could make contact with the senior God. Gnosticism and Christianity were interacting forces, each influencing the other. The more Christianity advanced, the more Gnosticism took over and adapted Christian doctrines and writings. Thus in Gnostic thought the figure of Jesus came to be regarded as an 'emanation' from the spiritual God; Gnostic documents added to the legends of Jesus and the apostles and attempted to claim them as its own. Gnosticism was a serious rival of Christianity for at least four centuries and, in some sense, it can be held to be still in existence in various fringe religious groups. However, it lacked both organisation and the universal appeal of Christianity. Gnosticism required hard study to be grasped properly. Christian doctrines, in their essence, are simple enough to be understood by the slowest normal mind but, at the same time, have implications so far-reaching as to have been capable of fascinating many people of high intelligence.

If, at a wild guess, there were 100,000 Christians in the world at A.D. 100, then a further wild guess would put their total as at least a million by A.D. 200, a tenfold rise reflecting the energy and enthusiasm with which their faith was being propagated. By A.D. 200 Christianity had become a recognised factor in the Roman Empire and historical uncertainties about it become very small compared with the vast uncertainties about its origination. The main centre was probably the city of Rome itself, but there were groups in almost every other city of the empire, particularly around the eastern Mediterranean. The great Church of Alexandria was just beginning its development. There were certainly Christians in France, notably at Lyons, and the faith had spread towards southern and western Germany. In all probability it had come to Roman-occupied Britain, although not until 303 is there definite evidence, with the execution of the Christian soldier Alban. Christianity was characteristically an urban faith; doubtless there were occasional missions to the countryside, where the majority of people lived, but most Christians were townsmen.

The New Testament existed in substantially its present form, although it was not conclusively defined until the fifth century, and Christian liturgical forms were being codified towards their present state. Compared with a century earlier, the whole thing was sobering up: such things as prophets, ecstacies and speaking in 'tongues' were held in lessening repute in mainstream Christianity. However there was a lively belief that miracles and faith-healing were continually happening. The canon of the Roman Catholic Mass was, in its kernel, already fixed. Christian bishops and priests did not wear vestments, as such, but it was customary to keep a special set of smart clothes for wear when celebrating the Eucharist. Ordinary fashions were to change but these clothes did not and, in stylised form, they are still in use. The Catholic priest vested for Mass today is wearing the garb of a lower class citizen of the Roman Empire in the second century: the main Mass garment, the chasuble, was a lower class overcoat used by those not entitled to wear the upper class toga. (One is reminded of modern parallels. The British Labour Party pioneer, Arthur Henderson, was also a Methodist lay preacher. When in 1924 the Labour leaders were summoned to Buckingham Palace to form a government for the first time, they were told they must wear frock coats, a form of clothing that was becoming obsolete. Most of them did not possess such things but Henderson had one because he needed it as a sort of vestment for his Sunday preaching.)

What were the rivals to Christianity?

The broad background to all religion of the time was the classical cult of the Greek-Roman gods, Jupiter-Zeus and so on, which can be termed paganism. The official cults of these gods and sacrifices to them continued although the educated had lost any simple form of faith in them. Some of the educated took the cynical view that the pagan cults, although untrue, should be continued as a method of keeping the ignorant masses in order. The same kind of argument is sometimes used today of Christianity. A more sophisticated view, influenced by Christianity, Judaism, Gnosticism, Greek philosophy and other forces, was that although the gods did not in themselves provide a complete explanation of the universe they did in some sense reflect or represent the supreme spiritual forces. This view put the gods into something of the position of saints in modern Roman Catholicism or of the 'gods' in popular eastern Buddhism. In terms of popular faith, the cult of the classical Greek-Roman gods was strongest in the countryside; the word pagan means, literally, a country-dweller.

Supplementary to the classical Jupiter-Zeus traditions was a newer cult of the worship of the Roman emperor. According to the stricter doctrines the emperor was supposed to become a god only on his death when he had his 'apotheosis', that is his taking his place among the gods. During the second century, however, and especially in the east, the custom grew up of worshipping the emperor as a god in his lifetime and temples were built for emperor-worship. The Jewish revolt of 132 was sparked off by a proposal to build a temple to the emperor on the site of the Jewish Jerusalem Temple. Emperor-worship is sometimes held to represent a corruption of the austere spirit of old republican Rome and so one of the forces leading to the fall of the Roman Empire but this is a view that needs to be handled carefully. Old republican Rome was highly religious and regarded its victories as the triumphs of the gods of Rome over other people's gods. Emperor-worship was at its height in the second and third centuries and was the cause of many Christian martyrdoms, the Christian faithful refusing to participate in a cult that was held to be necessary for the stability of the state. Men and women died rather than burn a single pinch of incense before the emperor's statue.

Then there were systems of thought which were as much philosophies as religions.

One outstanding group in this category was the Stoics, who derived from the teacher Zeno, who flourished in Athens in about 300 B.C. Stoic thought denied the possibility of knowing anything about God, even if such a being existed, but held that there was a natural order in the universe which should be examined in a dispassionate manner. This, obviously, is close to the attitude of modern science. People should be calm and unemotional and carry out their obvious duties. Stoics, like Christians, were sometimes martyred or committed suicide rather than worship the emperor. Pain and death were matters which should be treated with complete contempt. A more cheerful form of this style of thinking was Epicureanism, founded by Epicurus in Athens at the same time as Zeno was founding Stoicism. The Epicureans held that human happiness was the highest good and everything should be directed towards producing the maximum pleasure and the minimum pain. The Roman poet Titus Lucretius Carus (99–55 B.C.) developed the Epicurean philosophy and held that the universe consisted of tiny invisible atoms. In its popular form Epicureanism lost its philosophic content and degenerated into just ordinary pleasure-seeking and thus indistinct from automatic human behaviour. The more austere approach of the Stoics naturally had little popular appeal but Stoicism was an influential force among many of the most attractive Roman intellectuals. The Emperor Marcus Aurelius Antoninus (A.D. 121–180) was a busy Stoic scholar and his book *Meditations* is still today widely read. Many hold him to have been the greatest man who ever occupied the Roman throne. He persecuted Christianity because he regarded it as a politically dangerous superstition. Another Stoic was the philosopher Lucius Annaeus Seneca who was born probably in the same year as Jesus of Nazareth: Seneca's literary work, also, is still widely read. He committed suicide at the command of the Emperor Nero; he did it calmly and in a dignified manner at the end of a dinner party at which he talked to his friends for the last time. The spirit of Stoicism is still a force among a few in the world today.

Another category of religions altogether were new cults which were sweeping across the Roman Empire from the east. They represented, on the whole, a much more modern type of religion than classical paganism. Many of them were 'mystery' religions because they had esoteric doctrines known only to full initiates. To some extent Christianity must be included in this broad category in that only instructed and baptised people were allowed to attend the full Eucharist. Until a revision in 1968, the words of the Roman Catholic Mass referred to the consecrated wine as 'the mystery of faith', this coming in the actual formula of consecration. Yet in neither the gospel nor the Pauline accounts of the institution of the Eucharist do they occur; these call the consecrated wine 'the new covenant', which is not the same thing as a 'mystery'. How did the words get in? It cannot have been by accident and they date for certain back to the fifth century and, in all probability, back to the very earliest Christian worship, perhaps earlier even than the gospels. Judaism, too, must at least broadly be included in the 'mystery' category. To outsiders its teachings could look mysterious and some of the Jewish sects, although now rapidly dying out, had doctrines which they deliberately concealed from outsiders.

By the middle of the second century, however, Judaism had ceased to be a serious rival to Christianity. After the terrible disappointments of the failure of the Jewish rebellions and the non-appearance of the Christ, Judaism in the second century was drawing in upon itself and ceasing to be a proselytising religion. While it continued as an empire-wide force, and until at least A.D. 200 probably stronger than Christianity in terms of numbers, the priority of the rabbis was quality rather than quantity. What mattered was to preserve and strengthen the core of Jewish law and teaching now that the faith had no physical centre in the Jewish Temple. Keeping and defining the faith was more important than winning converts who, indeed, were liable to dilute it by bringing in alien ideas. Obviously it was not easy to keep Judaism pure when there were so many rival religions around but the rabbis, whose main base was now Jesus's homeland of Galilee, refined and narrowed Jewish teaching into a single orthodoxy. The Talmud, completed by the fifth century, put Judaism into substantially its modern, normative form. It was a much narrower Judaism than that of the time of Jesus; such extravagant sects as the Essenes had disappeared and so had the conservative Sadducees. What remained was substantially the Judaism of only one party, the Pharisees. It was as if today all the traditions of Christianity were to vanish save those of Methodism. Christian and Jewish ways of thought separated further and further apart and continued to do so until the nineteenth century.

Sex had always been an important ingredient in religion in either a positive or a negative form. Indeed the primeval religious feelings of mankind appear to have centred around fertility rites. Many of the rival cults to Christianity in the second century centred, in one way and another, around sex. For example the goddess Cybele was brought from the east into the Roman Empire. Her legend was that her lover, Atthis, had castrated himself in a fit of madness. What intellectual value the theology concerning her possessed is now impossible to judge but she certainly aroused high devotion in most cities of the empire. The priests of this cult felt so strongly that they castrated themselves in her honour and led processions through the streets to the music of drums, cymbals and horns. This castration complex had some slight influence upon Christianity. Taking literally the reported words of Jesus, 'If your right eye should cause you to sin, tear it out and throw it away',[1] some Christian enthusiasts, such as the theologian Origen (c. 185–254), castrated themselves to subdue their sexual desires. However this was only a peripheral practice.

A yet more interesting cult is that of the goddess Isis which had spread from Egypt across the empire and in the second century was stronger than Christianity and still powerful and growing. The main ceremony took place every spring and commemorated the death of Isis's brother-husband Osiris, which was held to have some atoning effect for people's sins. The priests of this cult heard confessions and gave absolution. Their spring processions, with the crowds carrying palms, fans and eggs, have an obvious kinship with some aspects of Christian Easter ceremonies. It is not too much to see in the cult of Isis the origin of the Easter egg.

The Isis cult was one which appealed strongly to women, who greatly outnumbered the men in it. The male equivalent was the religion of Mithraism which was probably Christianity's greatest rival of all. As late as the middle of the third century it might have been difficult for an impartial observer to predict which in the long run would be the more successful, Mithraism or Christianity.

Mithraism had a developed theology and a high code of ethics. It had sprung up, like so many other religious doctrines, as a derivation from the teachings of the Persian Zoroaster. It had a supreme God who had sent a lesser god, Mithras, into the world for the salvation of men. Mithras, a much more militant figure than Jesus, had slain a sacred bull, the blood of which washed away men's sins. There was to be a day of judgment on which sinners would be punished and virtuous people rewarded. The ceremonies of the cult included initiation by baptism in blood and a sacramental meal, and its leading officials were analogous with Christian bishops. Obviously Christianity and Mithraism interacted upon each other and, historically, it is difficult to establish who copied what from whom. Mithras's birthday was celebrated on December 25 and this may well have been a strong influence on the Christians in the fourth century settling on the same date for the birth of Jesus. (Earlier, Jesus's birthday had been very little celebrated and there is no historical clue to the correct date.) However, there was a central difference between the two faiths in that Mithraism was definitely a mystery religion; it had five grades of initiates and so it might take a man years before he had reached the inner teachings. Also the ceremonies of Mithraism were almost entirely for men, with women allowed only the most subordinate role. As a creed it appealed strongly to soldiers and merchants who took it right across the Roman Empire; in 1954 a Mithraist temple was dug up in the city of London, on the site now occupied by Bucklersbury House, and there is another one on Hadrian's Wall in the north of England. In some ways Mithraism, a brotherhood of men, was akin to modern Free-masonry, although it had a more sophisticated theology.

It is easy to conclude that Christianity succeeded in the long run because it was bisexual. Unlike either the cult of Isis or Mithraism it had a place for both men and women. Naturally men were in the leading official positions, as has almost always been so in human organisations, but, spiri-tually, men and women were equals and eligible on the same footing for the benefits of the atonement and the resurrection. It is difficult to read much in early Christian history without immediately being struck by the enormous numbers of stories about the work of women in supporting and propagat-ing the faith. The penetration of Christianity from its low class origins among slaves and freedmen into the middle and upper classes appears to have come largely through the con-version of women. Some, but not all, pagan husbands were tolerant of their wives being converted and allowed their children to be brought up in the new faith. Doubtless the husband would consider the local Christian bishop, with his shabby clothes, his appeals for money and his denunciations of fornication, a less than welcome visitor to his house but he would put up with him for the sake of domestic peace. The Christians also attached high importance to influencing chil-dren from their earliest years; to this day in Britain, for example, it is still the law that state schools should propagate the Christian religion and, in addition, all Churches run special instruction classes for children.

The anti-Christian writer Celsus gives a good idea of the pagan reaction to second century Christians as their faith went forging ahead. Unfortunately Celsus's work is not known in full but only through quotations of it in Christian works refuting it. However he had certainly taken the trouble to study Christian doctrines and scriptures and to look at Christianity in practice. While, in his descriptions, he was obviously trying to present Christianity in an unfavourable light, there does seem to be a certain flavour of authenticity to them.

'We can see them [the Christians] in their own homes, woolworkers and shoemakers and fullers—men devoid of all culture—who will not dare to utter a syllable in the presence of their masters, men of gravity and insight; but when they get hold of the children privately, they recount all sorts of marvellous things. They tell them to pay no heed to their father or their teachers, but to obey *them*; that the former talk idle tales; that they alone can teach them how to live and the secret of happiness. If they see any teacher or the fathers approach as they are speaking, the more cautious of them are alarmed. But those of greater impudence stimulate the children to throw off the reins, and whisper that they cannot give them any good instruction in the presence of fatuous and corrupt men who seek to punish them; but that they will attain perfect knowledge if they go with the women and their playmates into the women's apartments, or into the workshop of the fuller or the shoemaker.'

Of course to describe the propaganda methods of the Christians, their appeal to women and children, the excellence of their organisation and the vigour of their leaders is not necessarily to account for the whole causes of Christianity's success. Presumably it must be beyond dispute that Christianity contains factors of inherent human appeal. Its theology and its moral teachings correspond with some apparent human needs. The figure of Jesus himself, as portrayed in the gospels, is inherently attractive. The lack of information available about him, the lack of definition, has helped to give him a wide appeal through many different generations and in many different cultures. Anyone can use the raw materials about him to make up his own Jesus, suitable for his own time and place. We have had a Jewish Jesus, an anti-Jewish Jesus, a Roman Jesus, a scholastic Jesus, a warlike Jesus, a pacifist Jesus, a miraculous Jesus, a non-miraculous Jesus, a reactionary Jesus, a socialist Jesus, a liberal Jesus and other variations beyond number made by substantial thinkers. The unifying theme is the inherent attractiveness of this indefinite personality.

During the first three centuries A.D. very many people found the figure of Jesus so attractive that they were willing to suffer death rather than give him up. 'The blood of the martyrs is the seed of the church', wrote Tertullian. Certainly there can be no more dramatic proof of the impact of a faith than that people are willing to die for it. Christianity faced and passed this decisive test.

¹ Mt 5:29

X

The Seed of the Church

IN the ampitheatre at Carthage, north Africa, on March 7, 203, stood an aristocratic twenty-two-year-old girl called Perpetua. Beside her was her slave and friend, Felicity, who had converted her to Christianity. There had been a government attempt to purge the city of Christians but Perpetua, despite the appeals of her astonished and grieving family, had refused to abjure the new faith she had picked up from such a low source and had been sentenced to execution by being exposed publicly to wild animals. Mistress and slave entered the ampitheatre together. With them was a group of other Christians, led by the local bishop, Satyrus, and watching the scene was a crowd of thousands crammed into the circular tiered seating—the fact of Perpetua's youth and noble status must have added an extra spice for them to the proceedings. Satyrus died fairly quickly, his head being bitten by a leopard. Then an infuriated cow charged at Perpetua and Felicity. It went for Perpetua first and gored her badly but she, despite her wounds, got to her feet and tried to help Felicity. Meanwhile the crowd, in high excitement, was shouting such remarks as 'Enjoy your baptism!' Eventually the Roman governor, who had probably known Perpetua socially, got sickened at the battle between two girls and a cow and ordered his men to kill them by sword.

Christian witnesses of this unusually well-documented scene treasured the memory of it. To this day the names of Perpetua and Felicity are mentioned every time a Roman Catholic priest says Mass. The Christians not only accepted martyrdom but even gloried in it. Theologians debated whether it was right for a person virtually to commit suicide by voluntarily seeking martyrdom, or, on the other hand, whether it was all right to try to escape martyrdom by flight or going into hiding. The point was that martyrdom offered a certain entry into heaven and into unity with the heavenly Jesus. There was a special doctrine of 'baptism by blood' to cover those who were executed while still under instruction as Christian neophytes and before they had been received into the Church by baptism. Christians quite often sang hymns as they faced the wild beasts or the executioner; sometimes smiles were found on the faces of their dead bodies. Surviving Christians picked up pieces of the bodies of the martyrs, venerated them and said the Eucharist over them; it is still the canon law of the Roman Catholics that every altar stone must have the relics of a saint sealed within it. In Rome, partly for secrecy and partly for devotion to the faithful dead, the Church for nearly two centuries frequently worshipped in the catacombs, that is tunnel-like burial places cut in soft sandstone outside the city. They cut secret tunnels of their own until, in 258, the Emperor Valerian forbade the practice; his soldiers walled up two Christians they found in a secret gallery. The earliest known representation of the crucifixion is in the catacombs but it is a satire by some anti-Christian scribbler; it shows a man with a donkey's head fixed to the cross. The ordinary Christian emblem was not yet a cross or a crucifix but an outline drawing of a fish, which stood for Jesus's name.

Persecution continued intermittently for about 250 years, from A.D. 64 to 312. Its net effect was to strengthen not weaken the Church. It was not continuous — Christians had long periods of peace — and its incidence varied greatly according to local conditions. Most Christians, probably, did not suffer at all for their faith but the possibility always existed of a believer being arrested and executed; the total number of martyrdoms ran probably into tens of thousands.

The characteristic method of suffering appears to have been for them to provide sport by facing wild beasts in the arena but there were many other tortures and forms of execution. Laurence was roasted on a gridiron, Bishop Polycarp was baked, Sebastian was used by archers for target practice, Blandina refused to give in when her young brother was tortured to death before her eyes. The source of the courage of all of them was a remarkable faith in the elusive personality of Jesus of Nazareth.

The exact legal position about it varied but the fundamental cause was that Christians refused to acknowledge the imperial gods and the divinity of the emperor; this was held to be politically subversive. There was also a broader background of the Christians being in many places, apparently, disliked by the population at large. Their habits of withdrawing from much of ordinary society, of seeking new converts and of behaving with a humility that looked like arrogance easily caused unpopularity. Their meeting in cemeteries gave them a spooky air and they did, in fact, speak to the dead, believing that the prayers of deceased holy men could be enlisted on their behalf. (The full system and theology of prayers to saints was not yet developed—the word saint was the title of any Christian—but it is reasonable to suppose that the germs of it already existed.) Thus the Christians were natural scapegoats for anything that happened to go wrong in a community—a flood, a famine, an earthquake; the easiest way for a governor to evade his responsibilities was to blame the machinations of the Christians. The psychological processes involved were akin to those which later bred the classical form of European anti-Semitism. Since most Christians lacked Roman citizenship they could be put to death arbitrarily at the will of a local governor. (In 215, however, Roman citizenship was extended to all freemen in the provinces.) Imperial decrees, from time to time, made the persecution fully official. It was not so much the weaker or crueller Roman emperors who hit at the Christians

but also some of the more high-minded ones, men who
honestly believed that Christianity was a threat to civilisation as they knew it. The better the emperor, the more
eagerly he persecuted; the outstanding example in this
category was the philosopher-emperor Marcus Aurelius who
tried to eradicate Christianity because he considered it to be
a disruptive force. His attitude might be compared with that
of the more intellectual members of the Christian Inquisition
a thousand years later. Many local Roman governors took
pains to try to avoid executing Christians. Dialogues of
dignity on both sides took place as a governor tried to persuade a Christian to undertake the civic duty of burning a
pinch of incense in honour of the emperor.

A vivid case of an exasperated Roman proconsul dealing
with a strong Christian arose in the martyrdom in 167 of
Polycarp, Bishop of Smyrna, Greece. Then aged eighty-six,
Polycarp was one of the leading figures of the whole Church.
He had been Bishop of Lyons, France, and had preached in
Rome; he had known men who had known Jesus. During a
persecution he made a formal attempt to escape arrest by
exiling himself to a village outside Smyrna but he was easily
picked up. The followed dialogue between Polycarp and the
proconsul is reconstructed from a circular letter sent afterwards by the Church of Smyrna to other Churches.

As a preliminary, before it starts, Polycarp hears a heavenly
voice which says: 'Be strong, Polycarp, and acquit yourself
like a man.'

Proconsul: Remember your age and swear by Caesar's
fortune. Repent, and say, 'Take away the wicked.'

Polycarp: Take away the wicked.

Proconsul: Swear to Caesar and reproach Christ and I
will set you at liberty.

Polycarp: I have now served Christ for eighty-six years
and he has never done me the least wrong. How then can I
blaspheme my king and saviour?

Proconsul: Swear by the genius of Caesar.

Polycarp: It seems that you do not know that I am a Christian. If you want an account of what Christianity is, appoint a day and you shall hear it.

Proconsul: Persuade the people. [This remark seems to indicate that the proconsul was acting under popular pressure in persecuting Polycarp.]

Polycarp: I have offered to give a reason of my faith to you. We are taught to pay all due honour, except that which would hurt ourselves, to the powers and authorities which are ordained of God. But for the people, I esteem them not worthy that I should give any account of my faith to them.

Proconsul: I have wild beasts ready and I will cast you to them unless you repent.

Polycarp: Call them, then, for we Christians are fixed in our minds not to change from good to evil. But for me it will be good, to be changed from evil to good.

Proconsul: Seeing that you despise the wild beasts, I will have you devoured by fire unless you repent.

Polycarp: You threaten me with fire which burns for an hour and is then extinguished; you do not know the fire of the future judgment which is reserved for the ungodly. But why are you waiting? Bring forth what you want to.

The proconsul then sent into the arena a herald who proclaimed three times: 'Polycarp has confessed himself to be a Christian.' The crowd shouted back angrily: 'This is the father of the Christians and the overthrower of our gods; he has taught many not to sacrifice or to pay worship to the gods.' According to the account, the crowd, which included Jews, then contributed wood for Polycarp's burning. The mention of Jews in the account reflects the mutual antagonism between Jews and Christians which certainly existed.

The Smyrna letter ends with a gruesome account of the actual burning, the writer obviously being determined to relish it in every detail.

'... When the flame began to blaze to a great height, behold a wonderful miracle appeared to us who had the happiness to see it, and who were reserved by heaven to report to others what happened. For the flame, making a kind of arch like the sail of a ship filled with wind, encompassed, as in a circle, the body of the holy martyr, who stood in the midst of it, not as if his flesh were burned, but as bread that is baked, or as gold and silver glowing in the furnace. Morever, so sweet a smell came from it as if frankincense, or some rich spices, had been smoking there. At length, when those wicked men saw that his body could not be consumed by fire, they commanded the executioner to go near him and stick his dagger in him; which being accordingly done, there came forth so great a quantity of blood, as even extinguished the fire, and raised admiration in all people, to consider what a difference there was between the infidels and the elect; one of which this great martyr, Polycarp, certainly was, being in our times a truly apostolic and prophetical teacher, and bishop of the catholic church which is at Smyrna.'

Men tend to be cruel by nature and any political theory which does not take this into account is likely to fail if applied in practice. Public executions have continued in Europe into our own day and until the nineteenth century the punishment of hanging, drawing and quartering remained on the British statute book. People were burned alive, with Christian approval, at least up to the eighteenth century, including in England. Much of the public entertainment in the technically most advanced parts of the modern world consists of scenes of extreme violence and cruelty enacted in fictional form. It would be foolish, therefore, to ascribe exceptional depravity to the non-Christian inhabitants of the second and third century Roman Empire simply because many of them enjoyed watching Christians being executed in public. They had no films in which violence could convincingly be imitated by actors and so they either had to have the real thing or else go without. Public 'games', consisting largely of gladiators fighting to the death among themselves and against wild animals, were the routine form of entertainment in the

Roman cities, paid for often by rich politicians running for office. The Coliseum in Rome, built in A.D. 80 as a grand stadium for games, still stands; it can seat 50,000 people and has a circumference of a third of a mile. On occasion the central ring was flooded with water for the fighting of naval battles in which, in the cause of entertainment, gladiators died. Some of the marble seats, hired to the richer spectators, are now bishops' thrones in Italian cathedrals. Recent excavations have unlaid the elaborate system of tunnels, anterooms, and animal cages underneath. It is easy to stand 'back stage' in the Coliseum and try to imagine the feelings of a group of Christians waiting there to be thrown to the lions with 50,000 people cheering and jeering. However it should not be supposed that Christians were the principal or routine items on the Coliseum programmes. Like other criminals they were sometimes sentenced to die in the arena; for ordinary criminals of the tougher kind such a sentence had a sporting element in it—the man might actually win his contest and so his freedom. But the arena was mainly the province of professional gladiators who, by a combination of skill and luck, could sometimes raise themselves from slavery to affluence.

While few Christians have applied Jesus's injunction 'love your enemies' in any direct or literal sense, Christianity, like Judaism, is obviously opposed to killing people just for fun. When Christianity in the fourth century became dominant in the Roman Empire, the arena began to decline, the process spurred on by the general dissolution of order in the empire. However, it was two centuries before they were finally finished and the spectacle of the public execution of criminals has continued into our own day in Christian countries.

During the third century, Christianity made enormous progress. A tentative guess would put its membership at one million in A.D. 200; by A.D. 300 there is reason to believe that it had risen to some ten million, or about a quarter of the population of the Roman Empire. Between 260 and 303 persecution virtually ceased and the Christians began to flower out as a major social force. The first church buildings were erected, the characteristic style being that of the Roman basilica, a long hall used for public business, law courts and athletics. An altar was erected at the east end of a basilica with a seat behind it for the bishop. Christian scholarship grew up and there was much copying of the manuscripts of the New Testament. The intellectual centre of Christianity became Alexandria, which for centuries had been the home of scientists, mathematicians, astronomers and philosophers; from the Church of Alexandria every year was sent out a calculation of the correct date on which to celebrate Easter. The 'agape' or 'love feast' began to die out as the preliminary to the Eucharist. It was suitable more for an intimate group of enthusiasts than for large crowds, although it did not finally disappear until the sixth century. (In the twentieth century there have been some attempts to revive it in a new form.) The urgent expectation of the return of Jesus had faded and did not really spark up again until people began to speculate about it happening in the year A.D. 1,000.

Many Christians now were lukewarm and had come in for family reasons or for fear of hell; they often delayed being actually baptised until they were on their deathbeds, thus avoiding the obligations of full membership and at the same time getting a perfect passport for heaven since baptism was supposed to forgive all sin. Infant baptism also, presumably, was growing up in this period for the children of the devout, but it is difficult to trace how common it was. The normal method of baptism was by complete immersion. As late as the thirteenth century the font at Pisa cathedral was made big enough to allow an adult to be immersed. However, the alternative of merely sprinkling the neophyte with water was allowed—it must have been particularly convenient for deathbed baptisms. By A.D. 300 there were some places in the empire where Christians formed a majority of the population; their main strength was in the east and in southern Italy but they also stretched across France and into Britain. Three British bishops are recorded as attending a council in 314: the first prominent British Christian was the heretic Pelagius, an extrovert, red-faced man who by the end of the fourth century was preaching that there was no original sin and that people were saved or lost entirely at their own free will. Some of the legions of the Roman army, even, seem to have been heavily infiltrated with Christianity. The social status of bishops had ceased to be uniformly low and the episcopate began to include men of culture and education.

At the other extreme from the lukewarm Christians delaying baptism until their deathbeds there arose Christians who devoted their whole lives to religion. Celibacy was not a requirement for the ordinary clergy, although some practised it, but groups of hermits and monks appeared who gave themselves up to extreme ascetic habits. (Ordinary clergy at this time, it seems, were allowed to marry once but, unlike the laity, had to stay single if widowed.) The man normally reckoned to be the founder of Christian monasticism is Anthony (c. 250–350), an Egyptian who spent twenty years in prayer alone in the desert; he found the experience a difficult one and described how he was offered sexual and other temptations by demons. Eventually he founded a whole community of monks. In this early period Christian holy men seemed often to vie with each other in asceticism. To the ordinary austerites of fasting, flagellation, abstinence from washing and chastity they added such strange practices as seeing who could stand longest on one leg—one wonders, indeed, if there were any Hindu influences on them. One of the most celebrated Christian hermits was Simeon Stylites, a Syrian, who lived on top of a pillar which he got steadily made higher. For the last thirty years of his life he lived on one sixty feet tall and never came down at all—Christians would go out into the desert to get his blessing or just to gape at him as he prayed for hours on end, his outstretched arms silhouetted against the sky. He lived on vegetables which once a week the faithful put into a basket which he hauled up by rope. But such things were the first extravagant burst of enthusiasm; in the fourth century the monk Jerome (c. 340–420) combined monasticism with scholarship by producing from his cell at Bethlehem the Vulgate, the Latin translation of the scriptures which remained standard among Roman Catholics until the twentieth century. Settled monasticism, on approximately the modern pattern, came from the work of Basil (c. 330–379) and Benedict (c. 480–544); the latter set up monasticism in Italy and the west.

Heresy, as always, remained a matter of the utmost concern. Since Christians taught that a man could be damned through holding an incorrect view of the ultimate arrangements of the universe, it was of practical and not mere academic importance to get such things right. Even common danger from persecution was not enough to bring Christians of different views together. They excommunicated each other and refused to have anything to do with each other. Old Bishop Polycarp had been a friend of the heretic Marcion but on meeting him in the street in Rome after he had changed his views, Polycarp refused to answer Marcion's greeting; instead he stuck his fingers in his ears and said: 'I recognise the first-born of Satan.' Among the epithets used by Athanasius, Pope of Alexandria, against heretics were: maniacs, wolves, cuttlefish, atheists and eels. To this day Anglican clergymen are required to subscribe to the view that an excommunicated person should 'be taken of the whole multitude of the faithful as a heathen and publican.'

The leading heresy of this period was that of Montanus, a Phrygian who appears to have started off in religion as a castrated priest of the cult of the goddess Cybele and then to have become a Christian. In about 157 he gave himself out to be a new prophet, inspired by God whom, he said, played upon him like a bow upon a violin. Two women, Prisca and

Maximilia, left their husbands to attach themselves to him as prophetesses. Obviously to some extent Montanism was a reaction against the growing sobriety of the Church — prophets speaking in 'tongues' had been a commonplace a century earlier but now were falling out of mainstream Christianity. The original Montanus group settled down in two villages in Phrygia, in what is now southern Turkey, to build the 'New Jerusalem'; they predicted a new outpouring of the Holy Spirit which would complete the Christian revelation. They and the converts who travelled to join them lived in a state of high religious ecstacy, renouncing sex and marriage. It was the kind of thing which has happened over and over again in Christianity, especially in the nineteenth century. Montanus and Maximilia died before the new revelation took place but Prisca pressed forward on her own, the only woman before Joanna Southcott and Mary Baker Eddy to lead a Christian sect. The local bishops condemned her and she tried, ultimately unsuccessfully, to appeal to the Bishop of Rome. For a while, at the beginning of the third century, Montanism was a serious force in the east but gradually it degenerated, its salaried 'prophetical' clergy dwindling to a sort of fortune-tellers. (Of course all the available accounts of it are by its opponents so it is impossible to be sure what it was like.)

In the west, to which it spread during the third century, Montanism took on a radically different form. Instead of being associated with radical prophecy it became a puritanical, radical movement; it insisted, in particular, that nobody who had renounced Christianity under threat of persecution could ever be forgiven. It existed both inside and outside the official Church. Perpetua and Felicity, for example, were under Montanist influence but always have been recognised as members of the Catholic Church. The pamphleteer and historian Tertullian, on the other hand, appears to have joined a schismatic Montanist group. Probably in any given situation it was none too easy to distinguish which group was the Catholic Church and which was

schismatic; one later test was whether a Church was recognised by the Bishop of Rome but not all accepted this as the
correct touchstone and, anyway, it had not yet been
properly formulated.

Then there were heresies which were so far removed from
official Christianity as to count more as daughter-religions
than as Christian sects. Ultimately the major religion in this
category was to be Islam of which the founder was the
seventh century Arab prophet Mahomet. Mixing his own
revelations with Jewish and Christian doctrines, Mahomet
constructed a religion of durable force which, in the twentieth
century, is more effective than Christianity in winning new
converts. His book, the Koran, gives some apparently
authentic Christian traditions which otherwise have perished.

The third century equivalent of Mahomet was the Persian
prophet Mani (c. 216–276) who taught that Jesus had been
only a phantom and the bearer of only a preliminary
message. Quite probably Mani had never been a Christian
at all so the extent to which he thought it necessary to treat
Jesus with respect is an indication of the standing of Christianity in the world. Mani said an angel had given him a new
revelation of the eternal arrangements of the universe. There
was a conflict between 'darkness and light' (this is akin to the
Dead Sea scrolls and some aspects of Christian doctrines) and
eventually there would be a conflagration in which the light
would win. Mani himself, like Jesus, was a preliminary
'ambassador of light'. After travelling extensively, apparently
to India and China, Mani was martyred at the instigation
of the Zoroastrian priesthood of Persia. However his
organisation, Manichaeism, remained in existence and grew,
attracting, apparently, many converts from Christianity. It
had two classes of member — the 'elect' who were supposed to
live perfect and celibate lives and so be 'redeemers' of mankind and the 'secular' members who had to be just ordinarily
pious. The two classes were mutually dependent; an 'elect'
was forbidden to kill, so if, for example, he wanted a chicken

to his dinner he had to get a 'secular' to kill one for him. Manichaeism spread westwards across the Roman Empire and for a moment looked capable of becoming a major world religion. However, from the fourth century onwards Christian emperors persecuted its members to the point of death and it gradually dwindled, although small groups seem to have continued until as late as the tenth century or even later — the Albigensian heresy, which sprang up in France in the thirteenth century, had Manichaean undertones.

A more philosophic daughter-religion was Neoplatonism, of which the principal founding teacher was the Greek-Egyptian Plotinus (c. 204–270) who opened a school of philosophy in Rome in 244. Adapted from the teachings of the Greek philosopher Plato, Neoplatonism accepted the idea of a God on approximately the Christian and Jewish lines but denied that this God had revealed himself through any such person as Jesus. At most, Jesus had been only a saintly man. The way to approach God was through the exercise of reason, disciplined meditation and bodily asceticism. This, naturally, was a religion for intellectuals rather than for the masses but as such it won high influence, making many upper class converts from paganism. The Emperor Julian 'the Apostate' (c. 331–363), the last non-Christian to rule the Roman Empire, favoured Neoplatonism. However, as an institution Neoplatonism lacked a proper framework of organisation and it was finally suppressed by the Emperor Justinian in the sixth century, but meanwhile its influence had reverberated back into Christianity, notably through the mystical theologian, Augustine of Hippo (354–430). Brought up in childhood as an aristocratic Roman agnostic, Augustine went through a spiritual pilgrimage which throws a useful sidelight on the nature of his times and of the religious options that were open. First he became a Manichaeist, a faith which he practised and propagated in Carthage for ten years. Then he went to Rome and made a long study of Neoplatonism, becoming, at least for practical purposes, a member of that creed. Then, aged thirty-three, he entered Christianity and ended up as a bishop and active writer—he reckoned that he had published 230 books, and through them runs a clear vein of Neo-platonist thinking.

The final persecution of Christianity in the Roman Empire came with the reign of Diocletian and lasted ten years from A.D. 303. Probably born as a slave, he was an energetic self-made man who had won his way to the purple through the army and marriage. He was an oriental figure who cut himself off completely from the old Rome and ruled mostly from Nicomedia in what is now Turkey. He appointed three co-emperors to help him run the different sections of his vast domain. Diocletian's aims were to secure the empire from outside attack which he did with an elaborate programme for building fortifications and to improve its internal administration. Under the latter heading, he decided, must come the extirpation of Christianity. Except in a few cases in which Christians in public positions refused to co-operate, Diocletian avoided executions; presumably he hoped that relatively mild methods would be more effective than cruel ones which would make the public sympathise with the now powerful Christian community.

Diocletian wrought lasting damage to history by seizing and burning as many Christian manuscripts as his agents could discover or force the Christian authorities to surrender. Tens of thousands of documents must have disappeared in this way, many of them completely. What survived did so more or less by chance, except in so far as the basic documents of the New Testament were probably especially well guarded by the Christians and anyway were too numerous to eliminate completely. However, any historian of early Christianity must recognise that the bulk of documentary evidence was destroyed and that what remains is only bits and pieces. The hope must be that something analogous to the Dead Sea scrolls will turn up, that is a really sizeable

Christian library which was buried in some airtight place to preserve it from Diocletian's agents.

Every Christian was liable to be required by Diocletian's agents to produce a certificate that he had sacrificed to the pagan gods. Some of these certificates — *libelli* — are still extant. A Christian without a certificate was liable to be mutilated and sent into slavery, usually in the mines. The characteristic form of mutilation was to have the right eye gouged out with a sword and the leg tendons cut. Many of the new generation of Christians, including even some bishops, found this too much and yielded to Diocletian's demands. Some, ingeniously, bribed a magistrate to give them a certificate even though they had not actually sacrificed to the gods — moral theologians worried endlessly over the rights and wrongs of doing this. But very many Christians, as before, refused to give in and suffered the new form of martyrdom.

Apart from the serious loss of documents, Christianity as a whole did not suffer too much from Diocletian's attempt to suppress it — he himself more or less admitted failure and retired from the throne to devote himself to his books. Christianity was now the biggest cult in the empire, apart from the largely formal worship of the pagan gods, and so long as it did not collapse easily in face of persecution it was bound to win through.

In a complicated situation following Diocletian's retirement, the co-emperors fought with each other for control. From this conflict the son of one of them, Constantine, emerged the victor. His mother Helena, by extravagant legend a daughter of the English Old King Cole of Colchester, was probably already a Christian and had exerted some influence over him. On the day before the decisive battle in 312, that of Milvian Bridge just outside Rome, which gave him mastery of the Roman Empire, Constantine said he saw a flaming cross in the sky with the words 'In this sign conquer.' After consulting Christian clergy accompanying his army, Constantine removed the pagan eagles from the military standards and put in their place a monogram of the word Christ.

Thus the emblem of a man whose most striking teaching had been 'Love your enemies, do good to them that hate you', achieved its first secular triumph by being used as a battle mascot.

The following year, 313, Constantine issued the Edict of Milan giving toleration to all religions. Christianity had won, and apart from serious rivalry with Islam, continuing into our own day in Africa, became for many centuries the world's most successful religion at winning new converts.

XI

Strange Victory

THE Emperor Constantine the Great (*c.* 274–337) was in many ways a surprisingly modern personality, having much in common with the more robust and emotional type of industrial tycoon. He had a thick neck, a tremendous glare and a trick of throwing his head back like a lion. He lived well and dressed carefully, in his later years becoming corpulent. He threw himself with fanatical single-mindedness into whatever happened to be important at any given moment. His voice could be gentle and cajoling, his actions very rough indeed—he executed his wife and one of his grandsons. Occupying the throne as much from the result of his own efforts as from his birth, he had to fight to keep power. First proclaimed emperor at York, England, he won the allegiance of the local legions and then, under the Christian emblem, seized Rome and ultimately extended his authority to the eastern empire. His outlook was as wide as Europe—he had been born at Nish, in what is now Yugoslavia; he had been brought up largely in Britain; he ruled in Rome and founded the new city of Constantinople on the Bosphorus; he died at Nicomedia in what is now Turkey. He could be a rough man but he was not inherently cruel; his executions were political rather than petulant or sadistic. He had a hunger for power and he wanted to cut a great figure to posterity.

In such a man it is difficult to disentangle true belief from political tactics, especially as a measure of plain superstition was mixed in as well. Constantine was delighted that with

the Christian emblem on his battle standards he had won the
Roman Empire. He took a close superficial interest in the
Christian Church, which by any reckoning was now a major
force, and, apparently without opposition, took a large
measure of control over its affairs. However, for a long time
he had only the vaguest understanding of its teachings and
seemed to muddle it up with sun worship. He was not
baptized until he was on his deathbed. (This was a common
practice at the time, especially among well-to-do converts.)
In the last ten years of his life, however, he made a detailed
study of Christian teaching and, although unbaptized, took
to preaching sermons to audiences that included bishops.

The willingness of Christian bishops to co-operate with
Constantine was characteristic of the faith founded by Jesus
of Nazareth. Some, in recent years, have found social
revolutionary implications in the New Testament but these
cannot stand up to scholarly analysis. Only by taking particular passages out of context can Jesus's reported sayings
be equated with social revolution. The main Christian tendency, explicitly stated in the New Testament, is to accept
political authority and to try to work with it. (That is until
Jesus comes back in glory and nobody has a choice.) The
German clergy who during the Second World War gave
spiritual services to the troops of Adolf Hitler and, save in a
few heroic cases, refrained from political opposition to him,
despite his plainly unchristian beliefs, were well within the
mainstream Christian tradition.

Although the Christians might well have ultimately won
without him, Constantine did offer concrete benefits. In his
time all that was officially allowed was 'toleration' but in
practice Christianity became the main religion, a position it
still holds in Europe and European-settled countries. He
built churches for the Christians and encouraged them to
seek converts. The biggest enterprise of his life was to found
Constantinople, the splendid new capital for the eastern
Roman Empire; unlike old pagan Rome, the new city was to

be a specifically Christian place. His design worked well. In the centuries after his death, old Rome was overwhelmed by pagan, barbarian invaders whom it took more centuries to convert to Christianity. The eastern empire, centred on Constantinople remained a stable centre of Christian civilisation for more than 1,000 years after Constantine's death. At any time up to the fifteenth century, an impartial onlooker might easily have regarded Constantinople and the east as the obvious heart of the Christian religion.

Hardly had Constantine started on his patronage of the Christians than he discovered that they were split by a vigorous dispute originating in Egypt.

It arose over a difficult point about the nature of Jesus. Had Jesus, as God's Son, always existed or had he been created by God the Father at some definite point of time? Modern theologians would probably tend to regard such a thing lightly, if it were put to them as a new problem. Since the Father-Son description of God is obviously an analogy based upon human life, it cannot be pressed too far without becoming ridiculous. This is true of all analogies. Such reasoning, however, did not occur in fourth century Christianity.

The propagator of the view that the divine Jesus had been created at some definite point of time was the presbyter, Arius of Alexandria (*c.* 256–336). A tall thin man, Arius writhed as he talked and was notedly successful as a preacher to women. His enemies compared him to a snake. He delighted in discussing the inner nature of God and about how, at some enormously remote moment in the past, aeons ago, God the Father had created Jesus the Son. In opposition to him stood the archdeacon Athanasius (*c.* 298–373), a man of tiny stature, who had been an enthusiastic Christian since, as a child, he had played at administering baptism to his schoolmates on the seashore. In his 'teens he had followed the hermit Anthony to the desert and in his early twenties his brilliance had impressed the aged Pope of Alexandria into making him his archdeacon, that is his executive assistant. Eventually, at the age of thirty, Athanasius succeeded to the see himself. Athanasius preached eloquently against Arius, claiming that it lessened the dignity of Jesus to say that he had not existed for all eternity.

From Alexandria the argument, sometimes accompanied by violence and rioting, spread across the whole Christian Church. Since the Christians attached crucial importance to what a person believed, this was almost bound to happen in a dispute which involved the Godhead itself. The doctrine of the Trinity—that is of the Christian God being at once a single being on the Jewish model but also three persons, Father, Son and Spirit—had grown up during the second century and been often used in the third century but had never been formally defined. It does not appear in any exact form in the Christian scriptures.

The Emperor Constantine, interested and puzzled, decided that the way to settle the dispute was to call a conference of all the Christian bishops. It was to meet at Nicea (now Iznik in Turkey) in May 325. He himself would preside. For all his autocracy in ecclesiastical affairs, Constantine did not, apparently, consider himself competent to rule on the dispute on his own initiative.

The Council of Nicea was the first assembly of the leaders of Christianity. There had been local synods and councils before but none that had taken in the whole Church; until the imperial patronage a general council would have been administratively difficult to run and also dangerous. Christianity had grown up in local Churches; there had been some travelling preachers, some correspondence and a custom of a Christian travelling from one city to another with a letter of introduction but the formal links had been slight. The Council of Nicea was the first drawing together of the Christian religion as a single force.

Their expenses paid by Constantine, the bishops set off for Nicea, the ones from the more remote places taking weeks on

the journey. The official allowance covered two presbyters
and three slaves for each bishop. Some, however, seem to
have travelled more lightly and there is a charming report
about Bishop Spyridion of Cyprus, an uneducated former
shepherd. He set off for the council on a white mule, with his
deacon beside him on a chestnut one. On the way he met
some other bishops who thought he was so simple that he
could not be trusted to take part in the deliberations. At
night they cut off the heads of both animals. In the morning
Spyridion, unabashed, ordered the deacon to put the heads
back on the mules which, by a miracle, were restored to life.
The deacon made a mistake and affixed the white head to the
chestnut mule and the chestnut head to the white one, which
much discomfited the other bishops when this pair caught
up with them again.

Altogether, about 300 bishops took part in the Council of
Nicea. (The number is slightly suspect because theologians
immediately began to explain it symbolically, saying that
318 had attended because this was the number of the slaves
of Abraham.) They varied greatly in character and to a
superficial eye must have looked like a crowd of weird
eccentrics the reason for whose gathering could not possibly
be guessed. They had little of the uniformity of culture,
education and background that exists in modern episcopal
meetings.

Some of the older ones had been physically broken; they
limped along with horrible scars where their right eyes had
been. Some wore the wild dress of hermits, including the
goatskinned Bishop Jacob of Nisbis who was said to be able
to raise hordes of gnats against his opponents. There was a
blond Goth from Germany and a dark Persian from India.
There were elegant scholars such as Bishop Eusebius of
Caesarea, deep in Constantine's confidence and so the first of
the courtier-prelates. Eusebius's opponents could always
crush him, however, by reminding him how he had once
sacrificed to the pagan gods rather than suffer mutilation

under Diocletian. There was Bishop Nicholas of Myra, a plump man, jolly but short-tempered, the original of Santa Claus. Perhaps the first of the 'muscular Christians', Nicholas so lost patience with Arius that he advanced across the conference hall and boxed him on the ear. Tense and active in the lobbying stood the little twenty-five-year-old Athanasius. Bishop Sylvester of Rome had been too old to travel to the council but he had sent two representatives whose exact status, many centuries later, was much to worry papal and anti-papal theologians. There were no British taking part.

To most in the council it must have seemed scarcely credible that they were meeting under the chairmanship of the Emperor of Rome, symbol of a system which had persecuted their faith for nearly three centuries. Constantine, wearing his imperial purple with a foppish wig on his head, stared back at the bishops, darting his eyes from one to another. In 300 years (about as long as it is now since Oliver Cromwell) the faith they represented had conquered Rome. What had he let himself in for? He kept a control over the proceedings but did little talking himself.

It had been expected, not least by the courtier Eusebius, that Arius would carry the council. In fact, Arius and his supporters appear to have overreached themselves by being too dogmatic. Arius went so far as to start to sing songs he had written to popularise his doctrine among the masses; as he jigged up and down intoning: 'God was not always Father; once he was not Father; afterwards he became Father' the simpler bishops raised their hands in horror. It was possibly during the songs that Nicholas became so irate.

By an overwhelming majority (the exact figures are not clear) the bishops accepted a creed which repudiated Arius's doctrines; it was the first creed ever intended to be binding upon all the Churches and, with adaptations accepted at the Council of Chalcedon a century later, the Nicene creed is still the standard statement of orthodox Christianity. It marks the final development of the personality of Jesus of Nazareth from a Jewish teacher preaching on the Jewish Christ into the God of the Emperor of Rome. In the translation used in the Anglican Book of Common Prayer, he becomes 'one Lord Jesus Christ, the only-begotten Son of God, Begotten of his Father before all worlds, God of God, Light of Light, Very God of very God, Begotten, not made, Being of one substance with the Father, By whom all things were made: Who for us men, and for our salvation came down from heaven . . .'

Meanwhile Constantine's Christian mother Helena (*c*. 247–327) had been busy in Palestine looking up the scenes of Jesus's life, an enterprise which seems to have interested seriously nobody important before. She found that no trace existed of Jesus's birthplace or of where he had been crucified or where he had been buried. But she made up the deficiency with dreams, as a result of which the present 'holy places' in Bethelehem and Jerusalem came into being. Constantine had churches built over them. One of Helena's dreams resulted in the digging up of what was believed to be the actual cross on which Jesus had been executed, together with nails that had fastened him to it. Constantine used one of the nails as a bit for his horse's mouth and put another in his battle helmet. He abolished crucifixion as a punishment but it was to be another two centuries before memories had softened enough for Christians to use the humiliating execution instrument as their main symbol. Constantine was busily collecting relics of the Twelve apostles to lie in a church he intended as his own burial place in Constantinople.

Artists began for the first time to paint Jesus's portrait. They had no data to go on and had to use their imaginations plus what ideas came from theological speculation. The earliest tendency was to portray Jesus as an ugly man; it would be fascinating if it were possible to assume that this represented some shred of real tradition but in fact the cause was the Isaiah text: 'Without beauty, without majesty (we saw him), no looks to attract our eyes; a thing despised and rejected by men.' However this was unattractive and by the seventh century a council had ruled that it was 'unworthy, indeed impious, to represent Christ's features as contemptible or repellent.' For the last 1,500 year, at least, most portraiture of Jesus has shown him as good-looking.

In 337 at Nicomedia, Constantine lay dying and he at last sought Christian baptism, which he believed to be his certain passport to heaven. His attendants took off his imperial purple robe and clad him in the white of a Christian neophyte. Eusebius baptized him. Constantine urged his courtiers to rejoice because he was going to heaven. On Whit Sunday he died and the Christians carried him in a gold coffin to be buried in his 'Church of the Apostles' among the relics of the Twelve.

Back in the old Rome, the state priests enrolled Constantine with the other Caesars among the gods and offered incense to his statue.

But Constantine had devised his own title for after death. He made no claim to divinity but instead had 'Equal with the Apostles' inscribed upon his tomb; in that kind of claim lay much of the future of the worship of Jesus of Nazareth.

Appendix: Notes on the New Testament

THE New Testament consists of twenty-seven 'books' of which about half are attributed to the authorship of Paul of Tarsus or describe his career. The four gospels, which are the nearest thing available to a primary source on Jesus's biography, account for about forty-three per cent of the New Testament text. Nothing at all exists, however, attributed to Jesus's direct authorship. Material dealing with Paul or attributed to his authorship accounts for about forty per cent of the New Testament. The residuary material consists of a short account of the early Jerusalem Christians, letters attributed to Jesus's brother James and the apostles Peter and John, and the visionary Book of Revelation.

The original New Testament text was in the Greek language throughout with the insignificant exception of a very few words attributed to Jesus being given in the Aramaic he would normally have used. Behind the Greek texts may, conceivably, lie in some cases originals, now lost, in Hebrew or Aramaic. In particular, it is frequently held that Matthew may have been drawn up, in part, from a Hebrew or Aramaic original. But this can be only a matter of speculation. At the other extreme, Paul of Tarsus, although he would have learned Hebrew in the course of rabbinical studies, certainly wrote directly in Greek, his ordinary daily tongue.

The collection of documents, with the traditional names of the authors, cohered into its final form in the fifth century A.D. The only doubtful point, until the beginnings of modern

scholarship in the eighteenth century, was the authenticity
of the Epistle to the Hebrews as a Pauline document. The
distinction between the New Testament documents and the
mass of other early Christian material is, firstly, an obvious
chronological one. The New Testament, on the whole, is
older than anything else. Secondly, and more significantly,
the New Testament documents, with the possible exception
of the gospel of John, are profoundly Jewish in style, tone and
content and must belong to a period when Christianity was
a Jewish sect rather than a separate daughter religion on its
own. Of course the birth stories in Matthew and Luke sound
most un-Jewish but they could very easily have been added
by non-Jewish hands—in Matthew's case by minor amend-
ment and in Luke's by the insertion of a new, long passage,
complete with early Christian hymns. (Alternatively if such
material really did belong to the Jewish sect period, it
indicates how that sect possessed the seeds of a separate
religion.) All other Christian literature apart from a little of
the very modern stuff and, also, such borderline documents
as the Epistle of Clement and one or two of the 'apocryphal'
gospels, which failed to get into the Christian canon, is
profoundly non-Jewish in tone. This is to say that virtually
all Christian authors of the post New Testament period have
been Gentile in their approach rather than Jewish. This does
not mean that they necessarily lacked knowledge of the Old
Testament but that they approached the Old Testament in
an un-Jewish manner and, generally, were ignorant of
Judaism as a living faith. Indeed they tended to hold that
Judaism had no right to continue to exist and that the Christian approach to the Old Testament was the only legitimate
one. (Not surprisingly, Jews regarded this as an imperti-
nence.) At the risk of irrelevancy or undue repetition, the
point must be stressed here, because it is so crucial, that the
Old Testament, on its own, is nearly as inadequate for acquiring an understanding of Judaism as it would be for acquiring
an understanding of Christianity. To get back to the point,

the Gentile Christians, in formulating their sacred scriptures, were confronted with two types of document, Jewish and non-Jewish. They had ceased to be able fully to understand the Jewish ones and thus it is easy to follow a psychological process by which the Jewish ones, precisely because they *were* mysterious in tone acquired an oracular status in Christian eyes. One expects messages from an oracle to be in code and sometimes hard to understand. Added to this was the fact, and the rationalisation, that the New Testament authors appeared either to have known Jesus personally or (Luke) to have spoken to people who knew him, or (Paul and the author of Revelation) to have received special visions. This, again, gave the New Testament documents a special status. It must also be added, to avoid failing to see the wood for the trees, that for all the obscurities and inconsistencies in the New Testament, the documents contain passages which for sheer literary power at least approach the best in the Old Testament or, indeed, in ancient literature generally. One is dealing here with material that includes some masterpieces of ideas-carrying prose.

For many centuries after the definition of the Christian canonical scriptures, their status went on increasing. It came to be held that the Old and New Testaments had been written under miraculous divine guidance and thus were infallible. (Judaism, which of course, regarded the Old Testament as divinely inspired, concentrated much more on its 'sacredness' than upon its 'infallibility'.) The idea of a Christian miraculous Bible reached its climax in Western Europe in the sixteenth century at the time of the Protestant Reformation, which coincided with the invention of printing. The Protestant side insisted that the Bible was both infallible and the only legitimate source of doctrine. The Roman Catholics agreed that the Bible was infallible but said that ecclesiastical tradition was also crucially significant.

The decline of the Bible, as an infallible collection, began in the nineteenth century when, for the first time, the documents were subjected to scholarship of a scientific type. The work was mostly German to begin with, and such technical terms as 'Q', which stands for *Quelle*, meaning source, are still often expressed in the German language. Such analysis of the documents, combined with new archaeological, biological and astronomical evidence on the origins of humanity and the nature of the universe had by the early twentieth century severely shaken faith in the infallibility of the Bible. For a while the Roman Catholics rather than the Protestants were the leading defenders of the traditional infallibility of the texts but with the publication, with official authorisation, of the Jerusalem Bible in French in 1961 the Roman Catholics dropped this position and, in most matters of substance, now hold the same viewpoint on the documents as liberal Protestants. A few fringe sects, such as Jehovah's Witnesses and the Exclusive Brethren, still base their activity on the ingenious interpretation of biblical texts regarded as infallible. Some others, such as the Salvation Army and the Church of Jesus Christ of Latter Day Saints still formally profess belief in the infallibility of the texts, but in practice those of their members who have gone into the subject adopt a more liberal position.

Broadly, it is generally held today that the New Testament documents, or many of them, may be of high doctrinal or devotional value but need to be handled with grave caution on historical matters. They are held to be the voice of some very early Christians rather than the direct voice of the deity. Indeed this is about the only point on which all experts are unanimous. (Of course experts who believe in Christianity think that there was some degree of divine guidance short of infallibility.)

There are, broadly, three streams of thought on the nature of the New Testament.

The first has very little backing from advanced scholars but is worth expressing briefly because it reflects the views of many lay Christians and, even, many clergy. It can be called the 'face value' theory.

It is that three of the gospels were written by men who had known Jesus personally. The author of Matthew was Matthew the tax collector who had given up his job to follow Jesus. He wrote primarily for a Jewish readership and was at pains to argue that Jesus's life fitted Jewish prophecies. On this 'face value' theory, it is held that his style reflects that of a tidy bureaucrat or book-keeper, accustomed to precision in the use of figures and the arrangement of his material. Although his is the first book of the New Testament there are very strong doubts about whether it was really the earliest gospel to have been written. It is held that it must have been written before the destruction of the Temple in A.D. 70 and the most conservative views date it between A.D. 40 and A.D. 50; this was in an original Aramaic version, now lost.

The author of Mark, on the 'face value' basis, is held to be a young man, John Mark, who knew Jesus slightly and, probably, was present at Jesus's arrest. He is held to have become an assistant or secretary to the Apostle Simon Peter and that his gospel is based on Peter's recollections. This snags up on the point that Mark, unlike Matthew, gives no indication that Jesus conferred a special status on Peter; however, conservative commentaries get around this by attributing the omission to Peter's modesty. Mark's is the shortest of the gospels and is written in an energetic, untidy style. It has no account of Jesus's birth and only the briefest account of the resurrection. Mark's gospel is almost certainly the earliest to be written, at least the earliest in Greek, and must be dated before the fall of the Temple; some pin-point it to the time of Peter's execution in about A.D. 64, although, it is held, Mark must have thought about it over a period of nearly thirty years.

The author of Luke is held to be Luke the physician who travelled on missionary journeys with Paul. He was Greek, or perhaps Syrian, and very probably was of non-Jewish origin. He had never met Jesus but drew up his gospel by collating other written accounts and by interviewing such people as Mary, Jesus's mother. It is sometimes held that his professional training helped him to assess the evidence, particularly for the medical miracles. He wrote primarily with non-Jewish readers in mind and has the best Greek style of any New Testament author. Dating him, on this basis, is extremely difficult. Strictly he ought to have written his gospel before the fall of the Temple. But even the most conservative allow that in part he was copying earlier accounts and so it is not unreasonable to put him later, even as late as A.D. 80. (But, presumably, if he got the Christmas story direct from Mary, he must have done so well before A.D. 80 when she is most unlikely to have been still living.) Luke is also given as the author of the Acts of the Apostles which, in its present form, is incomplete, the final chapters having been lost or never written.

The author of John is held, on the 'face value' basis, to be John 'the beloved disciple' who knew Jesus extremely well. Even the most conservative agree that it is a late document and cannot be put earlier than A.D. 95. The explanation is that John wrote or dictated it in extreme old age while living at Patmos or Ephesus. In style it is highly theological and it is held to be an old man's reflections after a lifetime of consideration. John is given as also the author of the Book of Revelation.

The 'face value' view of the Pauline letters is that all except for Hebrews are authentic. Hebrews was, however, based on Paul's thought. To the considerable stylistic and other difficulties which exist over Paul's authorship of the letters to Timothy and Titus the conservative answer is that he was giving his secretary freedom to rephrase his thoughts and/or was old and ailing. It is commonly held that Paul's earliest letter to survive is First Thessalonians; this was written between A.D. 50 and A.D. 52. and is the oldest document of the New Testament. Extreme conservatives, however, hold that the oldest document of the New Testament is either Matthew or else the letter of Jesus's brother James which has been dated as early as A.D. 50. The letters of Peter and John are, of course, also taken as authentic.

A vast apparatus of critical scholarship has, during the past 150 years, almost totally upset the 'face value' theories as outlined above. For convenience, I label it the 'critical traditional' approach. While doubting the authorship and accuracy of the New Testament documents it maintains that, in the broadest outline, they can be taken as a rough outline of what happened. Even such central matters as the resurrection are questioned, but that Jesus lived, preached and founded the Christian religion is not. Apart from the habit of anonymous authors attaching the names of well-known people to their writings and allowing for their pro-Christian bias, it can be taken that the documents are intended to be accurate accounts and are not intentionally dishonest.

The habit of anonymous authors using the names of well-known people was absolutely routine in both the Judaism and Christianity of the period. It was a well-known convention and, like a modern advertising technique, it was a recognised method of getting a message over to the masses. Perhaps the gospels evolved from the authors traditionally given and perhaps not. It does not matter too much compared with the problem of examining the actual texts.

The 'critical traditional' method groups the first three gospels together as the 'synoptics' and puts the John gospel out on its own as the product of a separate tradition. The 'synoptics', obviously, contain a good deal of material common to them all. They appear to have three principal sources, in the generally accepted view. The sources were a primitive version of Mark, which provided the narrative framework and at least two collections, now lost, of the 'Sayings' of Jesus. The final Mark gospel springs from the primitive

Mark with extra, late material added at the end to supplement the resurrection account. This material, the final
twelve verses, is sharply different in style from the remainder
of the text and springs from a separate tradition of its own.
Some very early manuscripts include it but most omit it. It
was probably tagged on in the second century A.D. The
writer of Matthew worked with primitive Mark in front of
him, plus the collections of 'sayings'. The writer of Luke
worked in much the same way but had no access to Matthew.
There was some editing of all three documents, but by early
in the second century they had cohered into their definitive
form. Later editors felt none too free to remove obvious
inconsistencies—notably in the birth and resurrection stories
—but there were a few later interpolations. These include the
virgin birth story in Matthew, or rather the adaptation of
the Matthew nativity narrative to take in the virgin birth,
and the Matthew passage in which Jesus appoints Peter to be
the 'rock' of the 'church'. (This is the only mention of the
word 'church' in the gospels and thus does not ring true; the
idea of a 'church' is foreign to their ideology.) Paul apparently, did not use any of the synoptic gospels but, in
their present form, they must have been getting into cir-
culation by A.D. 100. The process was not a systematic
propaganda exercise by a centralised Church equipped with
a printing press. Until well into the second century few, if
any, local churches would have possessed copies of all three
synoptic gospels. By the end of the second century, however,
all the synoptic accounts were well known. There were many
rival accounts, the apocryphal gospels; these tend to be
heavy with miracles but may contain one or two scraps of
authentic information. However, the major weight of critical
scholarship has fallen on the canonical documents.

The writer of John has not used the synoptics at all. Since
he is late—probably well into the second century—and
primarily theological, the 'critical traditional' school for a
long time tended to devalue his historical standing. Lately,

however, fashion has tended to swing back in John's favour and he is no longer automatically dismissed whenever he disagrees with the synoptics. The origin of John, probably, is an enthusiastic theologian basing himself upon some now lost narrative which was not available to the synoptic writers.

The 'critical tradition' school accepts the authenticity of the first ten Pauline letters. The last three were written by someone else and attributed to Paul. The letters of James, Peter and John date from the late first to the early second century and thus cannot be authentic. The writer of most of the Acts of the Apostles could well have been the same person as wrote Luke but the first eight chapters, dealing with the early Jerusalem church, are radically different in style. The writer apparently had no access to the Pauline letters although he is only rarely inconsistent with them. The book must have cohered towards its final form at the turn of the end of the first century A.D. The Book of Revelation is a routine type of Jewish apocalyptic writing of the period. Exactly why it and the closely similar Book of Daniel got into canonical scriptures is not clear. Revelation is two separate texts combined by an editor in the early second century A.D.

The third stream of thought about the New Testament can be termed the 'revolutionary' approach. This used to be a crankish approach with oddballs trying to prove that Jesus was really Tibetan, that Christianity originally was connected with the Great Pyramid, or something else of that kind. It was also the approach of the more dogmatic kind of nineteenth century atheist who tackled the documents with the preconceived notion that Jesus was largely or entirely a myth. The 'revolutionary' approach, in its modern form, claims to be entirely scientific. It approaches the documents with detachment and attaches extreme importance to evaluating them in their historical context. Of course knowledge of this context has been vastly broadened by the discovery of the Dead Sea Scrolls.

15

The central problem, at present, is that of dating the documents. The statements about dating in the documents themselves—e.g. that Jesus was crucified in the time of Pontius Pilate—cannot be relied upon because that would be to presuppose that the documents *are* capable of being trusted on matters of historical fact. The only reliable method of dating them is closely to compare their linguistic style with that of material which has already been satisfactorilly dated, thus determining what could and could not have been written at any particular time. This may seem to be tenuous but in fact it stands up well in logic. To use a modern analogy, the most modest historian would have little difficulty in distinguishing, on style alone, between documents written in, say, 1870, 1920 and 1970. If he had some help, also, from the content of a document he would probably be able to pin-point it to the exact decade or even year. A document alleged to be a speech by Abraham Lincoln, would be a likely forgery if it included such expressions as 'scrapped', 'tough', or 'involvement' and a certain forgery if it had 'de-escalation', 'summit meeting' or 'gritty'. Of course the application of such procedure to the New Testament is a new field of scholarship requiring its own special expertise, and non-specialists are unable to grasp the detailed convolutions of arguments leading to particular conclusions. A supplementary problem is to get behind the Greek in which the gospels are written and back to the original Hebrew or Aramaic thought on which they must have been based. Also the Dead Sea Scrolls themselves are yet far from fully analysed and new scrolls are still being discovered. Final conclusions upon the New Testament are impossible until the scrolls are properly dealt with.

What matters is not so much the dating of the Greek documents, as we have them—they obviously spring from around the latter part of the first century A.D.—but the dating of the Hebrew and Aramaic traditions on which they are based. If, for example, it were to be proved that the traditions have to be dated at the early first century A.D., that would be a considerable underpinning of the traditional Christian position. If, however, they appeared to belong to a much earlier period, one or two centuries earlier, (or even only a generation earlier), the implications would be considerable and Jesus would thereafter have to be treated as much more of a myth. The study is primarily linguistic but the more radical Christian theologians are already working out a system by which God can be held to have influenced history through myths suited only to particular and transient circumstances and not necessarily of permanent validity. At what point such thought ceases to be specifically Christian and becomes mere Deism is a matter of opinion.

If the dating of the documents produces startling conclusions, the field falls open for an examination of the nature of the myth and the sect that nourished it. (It may be objected that the field is already open, irrespective of dating, and so it is, logically; but only a revolution in dating would be enough to upset the antecedent probability that Jesus was not a myth.) It would be fruitless here to go into the possible nature or motives of the original sect because, at the time of writing, very little work has been done on it of a kind that commands general scientific acceptance.

Whether or not any complete 'explanation' of the New Testament will ever be possible is unsure. Perhaps further work on the Scrolls, the discovery of the new scrolls and the submission of the whole available material to analysis with aid from a computer may one day produce a useful result. For the time being, they remain obscure documents in which many, at the devotional level, have found light.

Select Bibliography

Peter Ackroyd: *Exile and Return* (S.C.M. Press, 1968).

John Allegro: *The Dead Sea Scrolls* (Pelican, 1956).

Geoffrey Ashe: *The Land and the Book* (Collins, 1965).

Karl Baus: *Handbook of Church History* (Burnes & Oates, 1965).

Otto Betz: *What Do We Know About Jesus?* (S.C.M. Press, 1967).

Henry Chadwick: *The Early Church* (Hodder & Stoughton, 1968).

Haim H. Cohn: *Reflections on the Trial and Death of Jesus* (Israel Law Review Association, 1967).

Edward Conze (tr.): *Buddhist Scriptures* (Penguin, 1959).

Marcello Craveri: *The Life of Jesus* (Secker & Warburg, 1967).

Simon Dubnov: *History of the Jews* (Thomas Yoseloff, 1967).

Isidore Epstein: *Judaism* (Penguin, 1959).

Louis Finkelstein (ed.): *The Jews* (Peter Owen, 1961).

Helmuth von Glasenapp: *Buddhism and Christianity* (Buddhist Publication Society, Kandy, 1963).

Charles Guignebert: *Jesus* (Kegan Paul, Trench, Trubner and Co., 1935).

Charles Guignebert: *The Jewish World in the Time of Jesus* (Kegan Paul, Trench, Trubner and Co., 1939).

Charles Guignebert: *Ancient, Modern and Medieval Christianity* (University Books, New York, 1961).

Jean Guitton: *Great Heresies and Church Councils* (Harvill Press, 1965).

Christmas Humphreys: *A Popular Dictionary of Buddhism* (Arco Publications, 1962).

Alexander Jones (ed.): *The Jerusalem Bible* (Darton, Longman and Todd; Doubleday and Co., 1965).

B. J. Kidd: *A History of the Church* (Oxford, 1922).

John B. Noss: *Man's Religions* (Collier-Macmillan, 1963).

James Parkes: *A History of the Jewish People* (Penguin, 1964).

James Parkes: *The Foundations of Judaism and Christianity* (Valentine Mitchell, 1960).

Michael C. Perry: *The Easter Enigma* (Faber & Faber, 1959).

Chaim Raphael: *The Walls of Jerusalem* (Knopf, New York, 1968).

J. M. Rodwell (tr.): *The Koran* (Dent, 1909).

Hugh J. Schonfield: *The Jew of Tarsus* (MacDonald, 1946).

Hugh J. Schonfield: *The Passover Plot* (Hutchinson, 1965).

Hugh J. Schonfield: *Those Incredible Christians* (Hutchinson, 1968).

Wilfred Cantwell Smith: *Islam* (Princetown University Press, 1957).

A. P. Stanley: *Lectures on the History of the Eastern Church* (Dent, 1907).

Krister Stendahl (ed.): *The Scrolls and the New Testament* (S.C.M. Press, 1958).

Paul Tillich: *Christianity and the Encounter of the World Religions* (Columbia University, 1963).

Geza Vermes: *Scripture and Tradition in Judaism* (Leiden, E. Brill, 1961).

Geza Vermes: *The Dead Sea Scrolls in English* (Penguin, 1962).

Edmund Wilson: *The Scrolls from the Dead Sea* (W. H. Allen, 1955).

Paul Winter: *The Trial of Jesus* (Walter de Gruyter, Berlin, 1961).